THE MIRACLE OF PREACHING

THE MACMILLAN COMPANY
NEW YORK · BOSTON · CHICAGO · DALLAS
ATLANTA · SAN FRANCISCO

MACMILLAN & CO., Limited
LONDON · BOMBAY · CALCUTTA
MELBOURNE

THE MACMILLAN COMPANY
OF CANADA, Limited
TORONTO

THE MIRACLE
OF
PREACHING

By

JOHN EDGAR PARK

33052

✝

NEW YORK

THE MACMILLAN COMPANY

1936

PRINTED IN THE UNITED STATES OF AMERICA
BY THE STRATFORD PRESS, INC., NEW YORK

This volume contains the Lyman Beecher Lectures delivered at Yale University in 1936.

CONTENTS

CHAPTER I

THE MIRACLE OF PREACHING

DEAN SWIFT in one of his letters of 1736 writes: "I have long given up all hopes of Church or Christianity." This seems to be the opinion of the intelligentsia of all generations. The days of the church seem to them to be numbered: the church of their day is guilty of all kinds of stupidity and cowardice, it is ignorant and self-seeking, it is doomed. Yet the church and Christianity, like the British Empire, seem somehow to muddle through. Years after both the tombs and the dogmas of the intellectuals who officiated at the post mortem have crumbled into dust, the church insists upon flowering forth into great new buildings and great preachers whose voices, liberated by the radio, are listened to every Sabbath Day by millions; and legislatures and dictators are hampered in their schemes in all lands by solid bodies of church opinion, which they regretfully discover cannot be disregarded. The church has been a thorn in the flesh to the fashionable thinkers of every day, and to the selfish schemers of every age. It represents the common sense or spiritual view of life as opposed to the latest contemporary guesses of scientific speculation, or the conservative laissez-faire of the well-to-do. The church's views are generally those of a drowning man who hates to let go of the spar he is clinging to, till he is sure that the appearance of a life belt offered in exchange is really a life belt. Many of the life belts refused by the church in the past have been later proved not to be as real as the antiquated spar on which it was depending with ignorant common sense for life and salvation.

Ignorant as much of the church's opposition to scientific speculation may have been, yet its unwillingness to subscribe wholeheartedly to such endorsements as that in Pope's lines:

> Nature and Nature's laws lay hid in night,
> God said, Let Newton be! And all was light.[1]

may have had its part in keeping the door open for further and more accurate hypotheses. And Mr. Walter Lippmann has pointed out that modern psychiatry often reinforces with additional evidence the ancient empirical precepts of religion and ethics.

Those who have had much to do with the training of children and young people sometimes come to the conclusion that their natural normal reaction to any accusation or suspicion of wrong doing on their part is always a lie. This lie is an almost automatic reaction, a reflexive defense, and should not be regarded as having much moral significance. It is the next step that counts. So the natural, normal reaction of an institution to any suggestion or suspicion of change seems to be invariably opposition. The attitude of the church towards the new in each generation has been first opposition, then often toleration, and sometimes afterwards adoption. The period of opposition has however little moral significance, it should rather be looked upon as time for reflexion, for understanding, a fearful care on the part of a large body lest it be stampeded. The fundamentalists of every age in so far as they are sincere, are over-anxious passengers, half realizing that the train has stopped at a terminus, looking around in a serious manner among the gayly disembarking passengers to make sure that they have not left in their haste any articles of value in the car. The wisdom of such carefulness in changing cars is demonstrated by history. It would have been a mistake for the church to have capitulated too easily to the pronouncements of the physical science of the nineteenth century, seeing that in many ways the conclusions of the scientific thought of the twentieth century have modified even the most apparently objective deductions of the nineties. The new biology is in some respects more friendly to religion than the old physics. It is only when the first lie is persisted in that in the case of young people it takes on a sinister moral significance. Like a man whose house was lighted by kerosene lamps who refused to install gas in the eighties either because he thought the kerosene light was better or felt something better would surely come along, and later refused to install electricity for the same reasons but still lights his house by kerosene, so fundamentalism can, if carried too far, cease to be natural caution and become mere stubborn stupidity and egoism.

The bane of liberalism is the preacher who is always the creature of the last book or more frequently the last magazine article he has read, the bane of conservatism is the preacher who is hopelessly imprisoned in a system of phrases, the logical counters which he is afraid to lose because they are all he has to play with. The church as a whole picks its rather unheroic way between newly headlined certainties and old realized experiences, abused by those who are sure that the world is beginning today and by those who are equally certain it was created once and for all in B.C. 4004. Like most institutions the church often does the right thing or at any rate the wisest thing, but generally gives the wrong reason for doing it. Many doctrinal and symbolic reasons may have been given for allowing the use of incense to creep into the ritual of the Christian church, but the real reason of its appearance there was probably the gratification it afforded to refined senses in churches crowded by congregations of unwashed humanity. So, if one were to try to follow Pareto's method of objective analysis, one might conclude that the unnatural interest taken by the strictly orthodox in miraculous events was due not so much to the logical reasoning in which they feel those events have an all-important part, as to a suppressed desire for a poetical religion or a dim sense that mere goodness is, after all, not interesting enough or robust enough to be allowed to stand upon its own feet.

Theological bitterness is engendered by those who are mutually inspired by the best of their own motives to dislike the worst of their opponents' motives, while both parties see themselves as moved only by a single motive, that of loyalty to truth.

All bones grow from the ends. If you want to help a bone to grow you must stimulate its ends. Preaching is the growing end of the bone of religion. It is the point at which new matter, new experiences are taken into the fabric of the whole. Institutions, creeds, sacraments, rituals are the shaft of the bone, more or less permanent and fixed, capable of being used for many purposes, and strained in many directions. The preacher is at the growing end, he is thinking over and talking over with the people the relation of the old to the new, the modifications and additions to the shaft which will bring added leverage and new power to the old limb. The preacher is engaged in welding today into yesterday. Equally misguided are those who say the old bone is too short, let us discard it and build a new one out of the air of today, and those who say the old bone was delivered to us once and for all as perfect for our needs, let us continue to worry it! And how some of the poor old texts of the Bible have been worried by the dogs of the homiletical kennel!

A history of the Christian church has yet to be written which will in any adequate manner trace the origin of all the multifarious elements which have come together largely through the preaching of the past into the body of Christian faith and practice. One large contribution came from Galilee, another from Mt. Sinai and the prophets, but how many other elements from other faiths and races are blended to make up the presuppositions of even the barest and strictest and most orthodox Christian service! It may be that the nearest we ever get to the historical Jesus is in the preaching of Peter about him as recorded for us in the earliest gospels, and all later developments of the gospel are equally the results of these practical discussions held between preacher and congregation. Perhaps the preachers have had more to say than the congregations, but it has been in the interaction between them that the truths of the past have been ever modified to meet the needs of the present. Even the great church councils could not go further than the general opinion generated in the churches of the day through the combined thinking together of preacher and congregation. Some preachers think of themselves as proclaiming the truth to more or less unwilling hearers. Other preachers feel that they should be exhorters urging those who are unaware or unpersuaded to adopt new principles or practice. But most of the greatest preachers at their best have become the very mouthpieces of their congregations, expressing for them their better selves, the very voice of their inmost hearts so that the whole congregation found itself raised above its ordinary self, feeling and thinking greater things than it ever dreamed itself capable of before. If the hearer "once discovers that the preacher knows more about him than he knows about himself, he will willingly let himself be led on, impelled by his sense of need, and allured by the promises; and so he follows the minister till the thread breaks." [2]

The art of preaching lies in this carrying on of the thought and feeling of the people one step further than they had ever gone before. The pedant preacher develops his subject logically from a point where the people have never been to another point at which they never arrive, under such circumstances preaching becomes a pleasant game of sacred solitaire. The relation of exhorter to exhortee has become so unnatural a pose in modern life that the congregation senses something artificial and worked-up about the emotion of the orator, and stands upon the side lines interested in the exhibition but not impressed. But the power of whipping up the flame of thought and emotion from every individual in the crowd till a great pyramid of quivering fire envelops all, and the tongues of flame unite in one general conflagration reaching from earth to heaven, that is the true union of incandescent thought and feeling in a great experience of preaching. It is the result of moderate brains, meticulous preparation (often departed from at the moment of delivery), deep emotion and rich experience.

All true preaching begins with a lump in the throat, a catch in the breath, a sudden flash of insight, a new vision. In the study, on the street, talking with the plumber or visiting the sick, suddenly you find yourself rounding a headland, long the last boundary of your vision, and sighting a new stretch of coastline, new estuaries and harbors: an illustration by Doré in the old edition of *The Ancient Mariner* in your childhood home flashes on your memory with new meaning, and the words below it:

> The Fair breeze blew, the white foam flew,
> The furrow followed free;
> We were the first that ever burst
> Into that silent sea.

The following description of the experience of inspiration is not taken from one of the ancient prophets, but from the writings of one of the most gifted and one might say sceptical writers of the nineteenth century. If it may seem too high and lofty a matter for ordinary men to deal in, yet all true inspiration is, if often less intense, yet of the same nature as this great experience which he tries to describe as follows:

"If the slightest trace of superstition were left in one's nature one would hardly be able to dismiss the thought that one had become nothing less than the incarnation, the mouthpiece, the medium of tremendous forces. The best description of what happens is 'revelation,' in the sense that suddenly with unspeakable certainty and distinctness something becomes visible, audible, something that moves and stirs one to the very depths. One hears, one does not seek; one takes, one does not ask who gives. Like a lightning flash a thought blazes forth, as though by some objective necessity and with no hesitation in its outlines; the choice has never been mine. An ecstasy whose intensity often resolves itself into tears; an ecstasy forcing one to pace up and down, now in a storm of emotion, now in quiet reflexion; a condition of being completely beside one's self with the most distinct consciousness that even one's toes partake of the nervous excitement; a depth of happiness in which the greatest pain and darkness do not seem contradictions, but rather colors inevitable and necessary in such a cataract of light; an instinct for rhythmical relationships spanning vast realms of being whose reach, since the necessary demand for a wide-flung rhythm is almost the measure of the force of the inspiration, is a sort of adjustment between their compression and extension. Everything happens absolutely involuntarily but in a stormy sense of freedom, of independence, of power, of divinity. The automatic way in which the figure, the comparison, offers itself is strangest of all; one no longer knows what is figure, what is simile; each thing suggested seems the nearest, the correctest, the simplest expression. It seems in truth as if things came forward of themselves and offered themselves as figures. . . . All things come fawning to thy speech, for they wish to ride upon thy wave of inspiration. On every one of the figures thou ridest here to every truth. Here the words of all being and the shrines of all words open to thee; all being seeks to become word, all becoming seeks to learn speech from thee. This is my experience of inspiration." [3]

Even a far-off experience like to this does not come to the loafing idle mind, it is the result of long discipline, exact thought, toil, hardship, the sweat of the brow, but it generally descends upon one gratuitously as if unrelated to all the toil, at odd moments, entirely unexpected, a gift from heaven to a mind able to receive and hold it. After the study, the consecutive thought, the wrestling of the spirit, one goes out to follow the advice of Walt Whitman: "This is what you shall do: Love the earth and sun and the animals, despise riches, give alms to everyone that asks, stand up for the stupid and crazy, devote your income and labor to others, hate tyrants, argue not concerning God, have patience and indulgence toward the people, take off your hat to nothing known or unknown or to any man or number of men, go freely with powerful un-educated persons and with the young and with moth-ers of families—re-examine all you have been told at school or church or in any book, dismiss whatever insults your own soul, and your very flesh shall be a great poem and have the richest fluency not only in its words but in the silent lines of its lips and face and between the lashes of your eyes and in every motion and joint of your body." [4] Add to those instructions the touch of reverence and humility, the absence of which sometimes left Whitman's catalogues of sug-gested scenes too miscellaneous a hodgepodge of un-graded impressions, and you have an almost perfect description of the state of life of him who would prepare himself for some lofty spiritual insight.

One can trace this growth of inspiration in all the greatest sermons. In the year 1865 the curious fact that a drop of sour milk added to a pan of sweet milk turns the whole of it sour, but that a drop of sweet milk added to a pan of sour milk will not turn the whole pan sweet, that "you send your boy to college, and if he goes there pure you hardly expect him to purify the air about him. You only ask, with trembling lips, of God, that he himself be not defiled," this fact suddenly flowers in the mind of Phillips Brooks into the splendid sermon on "The Mystery of Iniquity." Twenty-two years later suddenly with new eyes he notices that one of the hindrances or obstacles which may settle around any object, and prevent anyone outside from reaching it, is the very substance of that object, hardened upon the surface and shutting up the body of the object behind and within itself, and thus was born the sermon upon "The Principle of the Crust." [5] If such inspirations do not come to you, it is because your mind is asleep. William Blake can hardly comfort you with his remark: "A fool sees not the same tree that a wise man sees." The fact is that there are preachers who make sermons, and there are preachers in whom sermons are born.

How can one tempt the vision? Reading for the purpose of getting sermons is the unpardonable sin against the spirit both of true scholarship and of true inspiration. Walking up and down the study floor, hoping for something to come, is generally wasted time. The manufacturer of imitation pearls says, "Go to, now, I will make a pearl," and lo he has imitation pearls, but it is when the currents and tides of the ocean are about their own business that true pearls are born. Preaching must be a by-product of life. Effort is not enough. Filing systems and note-books are of value in so far as facts are concerned and references, but as far as the real initial inspiration for a sermon goes, the used word is stale. Every day the manna falls, and it must be used today, it will not keep overnight. "An unexcited dog cannot bark." The secret of success is known only to those who have not succeeded. Yet there are indications, straws upon the surface of the hidden current which are of some value. Samuel Butler says: "Do not search for subjects, let them choose you." [6] Walter Pater speaks of "that interior, mental condition of preparation or expectancy." [7]

The writer was once present when a philosopher and a poet were discussing the question of inspiration. The poet said, "I have not been able to write anything for months. I have not been in the mood." The philosopher remarked, "If I were a poet, I should have somewhere a table and a chair and a pen and a sheet of paper, and I should sit there for a while every day. That at least would be a prayer." This is good advice, but it would be more likely to succeed with a philosopher than with a poet. The preacher who occupies a position somewhere between the philosopher and the poet, seeking truth and beauty less as ends in themselves and more as ways to goodness, can profit by it, only if his mind has been previously heated up by some exertion, or if he comes fresh from some daring experiment in living; for the preacher has constantly to remind himself that although he has so much to do with words, yet the religion with which he deals can only be expressed in deeds. Richard Baxter in the year 1658 refers in his book *The Crucifying of the*

World by the Cross of Christ to John Eliot and is
far from being, as some have thought, unconsciously
humorous, when he says: ". . . as Mr. Eliot and his
helpers find of their Blessed labours in New-England,
where if the languages and remote habitations . . . of
the inhabitants did not deny them opportunity of
speech, much more might be effected." Warmed by
study, thought, meditation, devotion or by some self-
discipline and practical godliness, the preacher can
come to his sheet of paper with some hopes of success
in his endeavors. The flash may come from familiar
regions, the Psalms or the Gospels or the Epistles of
St. Paul or may strike from unexpected quarters as in
the case of Phillips Brooks. First-hand observation and
experience give the highest types of inspiration, then
come the classics, those great works which stimulate
originality rather than plagiarism in the reader and
seem forever to dwell in an impregnable futurity,
least valuable of all are those suggestions which have
been previously worked over by one's contemporaries.
The sermons you paste together out of Phillips
Brooks' *Mystery of Iniquity* will not be as good as
one born of your own experience in trying to clear
your back lot of poison ivy.

But if reading for the purpose of getting sermon
topics is death to all true culture, the direct attempt
to find them in daily life is equally mistaken, and leads
the preacher's friends continually to humiliate him by
interjecting suggested homiletical uses for every trivial
occurrence of daily life. The patronizing remark,
"You could make a sermon out of that," continually

keeps the preacher in his place on the sub-human plane. Life lived for homiletical purposes is not life. The experiences of most value seldom occur to one as having symbolic or illustrative meanings till they are remembered afterwards as analogous to the spiritual and moral problems with which one is engaged in the moments of inspiration. The unreality of many sermon illustrations, the number of people whom many preachers seem to have seen with tears streaming down their faces, and the way in which these sinners play into the hand of the preacher by their easily refuted remarks and sudden capitulations or at least by the speedy nemesis which overtakes them, make one fear that the preacher himself is leading not a human but merely a homiletical life, for experience may be deformed by the desire to preach about it. It is true of all professional people but perhaps especially of preachers and teachers, that they must graduate into humanity before they graduate into their profession. Exactitude and thoroughness in some field of study is one of the best ways of keeping human for a man who has in other ways to spread himself so thin over so many interests and enterprises. Thus can he keep his self-respect in a world of men.

The subject matter of preaching has been frequently treated in other years in these lectures. The adverb rather than the substantive is the point of interest now. But it may be said in passing that all signs point to the fact that for our life today much of the previous content of sermons is irrelevant. Obedience to the god of the particular preacher, duty to God as interpreted

by a particular preacher, or his certainties as to God's
plans and ideas leave an intelligent listener cold, because his god may be different from that of the
preacher and he is not sure of the preacher's creden-
tials to represent God. But preaching which reveals to
a man his real self with its powers and weaknesses, its
foibles and depths, inner capacities of which he was
only dimly aware, and possible ways of gaining courage and poise, strength and peace, help him to find
and grasp the hand of the god, who for him is God.
The power of demonstrating this to the hearer is the
preacher's credential. Almost every movement which
sets out to do this for the individual has much to
teach the preacher and should be studied by him. All
of them claim to have the whole truth, because a part
of the truth always looks greater than more of it
would look like. "Beware of Imitations" is the motto
of all proprietary products. "Our blades only must be
used in this razor" is, however, a pleasantry taken
seriously only by the simple. Study all razors and use
your own blades in them. There is suggestion in Con-
gregationalism, Roman Catholicism, Christian Science,
Buchmanism, New Thought, Freudianism, Socialism,
YMCAism, and even in your own ideas. Among
these the writer is inclined to think that Congrega-
tionalism knows most about group inspiration, Roman
Catholicism about mass worship, Christian Science
about self-suggestion, Buchmanism about morbid loneliness, New Thought about cheerfulness, Freudianism
about complexes, Socialism about fair distribution of
goods, YMCAism about the clean body, and your

own ideas about how all such ideas work in your own life.

History teaches the preacher that the situation he is in is not a new one, that all the types of people he has to deal with, including himself, have operated in the world before with interesting results. Historical analogy is a more subtle weapon than exhortation. Both liberal and conservative churches might celebrate annually a festival week for their "wayside pulpits," during which they might relax the direct method of improving the public, and publish to the astonished populace certain less-known passages from the debates on progressive measures in the past. Lord Lauderdale opposed the first gas light bill introduced into the British parliament on the ground that a "most important branch of trade, our whale fisheries, would be ruined."

In the year 1807, a bill to provide elementary schools throughout England was introduced into parliament, and was defeated in the House of Lords. Both the Archbishop of Canterbury and the President of the Royal Society for the Advancement of Science voted against it, the latter arguing as follows: "However specious in theory the project might be, of giving education to the labouring classes of the poor, it would in effect be found to be prejudicial to their morals and happiness; it would teach them to despise their lot in life, instead of making them good servants in agriculture, and other laborious employments to which their rank in society had destined them; instead of teaching them subordination, it would render them

fractious and refractory, as was evident in the manufacturing counties; it would enable them to read
seditious pamphlets, vicious books, and publications
against Christianity; it would render them insolent to
their superiors; and in a few years the result would be
that the legislature would find it necessary to direct
the strong arm of power towards them, and to furnish
the executive magistrate with much more vigorous
laws than were now in force." [8]

Both Lord Lauderdale and this President of the
Royal Society are charter life members of almost all
churches. And conservatives could find almost equally
telling passages from liberal theorists in the past, if
they cared to look them up for themselves.

History freshly and accurately studied at first-hand
from the masters of the field or from the records
themselves, is, if the preacher's thesis is valid, one great
analogy, which is not merely pertinent, but organically one with the subject in hand. The opposition of
good men in the past to social changes which are the
commonplaces of ordinary life today, can, when retold fairly, be more effective than denunciation of
those who occupy similar positions today. "All our
hopes for the future depend on a sound understanding of the past." Nothing can be understood till one is
familiar with its history.[9]

The study of history will bring before the preacher
one of the most perplexing of his problems. Should he
aim to present objective truth, or must his art be that
of propaganda? Is he essentially a propagandist for
righteousness? It is an awkward dilemma. For there is

too little difference for comfort between two such
statements as these: This pronouncement may not be
absolutely true, but its effect upon the young in my
congregation will be in the direction of virtue, and,
These men may not have been guilty of the crime for
which we are condemning them, but they are a "bad
lot," and the effect on society of acquitting them
would be a more serious injustice than that of execut-
ing them.

Exact science is not so much help to the preacher
in this respect because scientists are not as yet as conscious as historians, that they are not dealing with
objective fact, but always with nature in a state of
man. A comparison of the letter which Lord Acton
sent to all contributors to *The Cambridge History* in
1898 with the *Conclusions and Recommendations of
the Commission on the Social Studies* of the American
Historical Association in 1935 is of interest as bringing this difficulty clearly to the attention of all teachers. Lord Acton said: "Our scheme requires that
nothing shall reveal the country, the religion, or the
party to which the writers belong. . . . Contributors
will understand that we are established not under the
Meridian of Greenwich, but in Long. 30° W; that
our Waterloo must be one that satisfies French and
English, Germans and Dutch alike; that nobody can
tell, without examining the list of authors, where the
Bishop of Oxford laid down the pen, and whether
Fairbairn or Gasquet, Libermann or Harrison took it
up." [10] The Commission on Social Studies Report may
be summed up as saying that while the community

will have to be convinced "that the infinitive 'to teach' does not mean to propagandize but rather to develop thinking," yet, "hitherto our prevalent philosophy has been that the school should be neutral on controversial issues, that it should present evidence from varied angles but withdraw from any partisanship which might explode social dynamite. The fear of such a detonation has usually operated to cause the school to stop amply short of social actualities. The Commission now seeks to close this gap between school and society by disavowing the ideal of disinterestedness." [11]

All life seems to tremble like an arc light on the horns of a dilemma. As soon as the foolish light decides definitely to choose one pole and discard the other, the result is darkness and death. The vibrations which constitute all teaching or preaching oscillate between the heresy of truth and the dogma of convenience, between fact and propaganda, between opinion and courtesy, between courage and humility, between the goal and the next step, between certainty and mystery, between the ideal and the practical. The preacher has no special privilege here. He knows Mr. Gradgrind's devotion to fancifully objective entities called facts and especially on Mondays is capable of delivering Mr. Bounderby's address. "As you all know me, and know what I am, and what my extraction was, you won't expect a speech from a man who, when he sees a Post, says 'that's a Post,' and when he sees a Pump says 'that's a Pump,' and is not to be got to call a Post a Pump, or a Pump a Post, or either of them a Toothpick." [12] But when confronted on Sunday noon with the indignant protests of "practical" men he also understands how Lord Halifax felt when as Sir William Temple records, he asserted "that the plot must be handled as if it were true, whether it were so or no, in those points that were so generally believed," and definitely stated: "this is not an age for a man to follow the strict morality of better times." [13]

Is there any possibility of a steady light emanating from the vibrations of a soul oscillating between the horns of this dilemma? An arc light does flicker. Yet it provides practical illumination.

All so-called objective facts are colored by human opinions and emotions. When a student in one of Rabbi Davidson's classes began a paragraph in his practice sermon with the words "humanly speaking," Dr. Davidson interrupted him with the question, "How would you propose to speak otherwise?" And the "will of God," the "divine law" also comes to us "humanly speaking." Our view of the existing state of affairs and the clear will of God in the matter can only be brought into a tolerable unity when we realize that our duty in the matter is neither to become cosmic director of affairs like the man

> Who seeing that the sun would shortly rise
> "Oh let me help!" he to the Creator cries

nor is it to acquiesce in things as they are. It is neither to save our own souls by telling people how the human race ought to be situated in the cosmos nor to save our souls by acting in the way most fashionable and popular at the moment.

The problem of the dilemma is not that of saving our own souls at all. It is the project of finding in present circumstances the best next step towards carrying out in things as they are the most hopeful movement, and aligning some small part of them in the direction of what seems to us the clear will of God. The preacher must be a propagandist on the basis of all the facts that he knows. But he must always remember that in selecting certain facts for emphasis, he is always rejecting or ignoring others. A judicious selection of facts can be made to indicate the goodness of God, another group of facts can be found to prove the indifference of God, and an imposing array of facts leaves no doubt in the mind of the collector of the badness of God. If the preacher is convinced that the first set of facts has more validity for him than the other two series, his conviction will carry more weight with his congregation if he shows that he is familiar with the facts of the other series.

The man who when asked if he believed in God answered, "Yes—No—Sometimes" had perhaps gone as far as most people can go "humanly speaking." But the minister has been selected by society especially to keep before it the "yes" mood, in so far as he and it consider that mood the deepest, wisest and most valuable of the three.

If I may cite my own case as an example: As long as this country had not gone into the great European conflict I followed Wilson in his attempts to be fair to both sides, to try to get both sets of angry nations to behave. I preached pacifism, I discounted all stories of atrocities by examples taken from the Boer War, I warned congregations that the first casualty in any war is truth, I encouraged benevolence for the wounded and suffering on both sides, much to the growing distaste of groups of the congregation at home. But when I felt that Wilson had played our game as far as possible in the world as it was, that he had boldly gone as far as any man in his position could go to proclaim and carry out the Christian ideal, then I told my congregation—he seems to me to have done all that can be done in a mad world. There is nothing I can see for him to do but to throw up his hands, resign and leave the country to the direction of others madder than he, or for him to declare war as he has done. But the church is not a recruiting station. Our duty is to relieve human suffering in this terrible catastrophe. The method our country is using cannot be reconciled with our religion. Jesus cannot by any stretch of imagination be found with a uniform or made to officiate with a machine gun. We may as individuals hope that the allies win and work towards that end or we may still continue to declare that the whole thing is wrong, and we shall have nothing to do with it. But as a church we must act as a hospital acts in a great epidemic of physical and mental disease, caring for our brothers in their desperate need and hoping and praying that out of it all will come some move towards ending such universal suffering in the future. I still wonder whether I was a wise man or a coward.

The preacher must make it clear to himself and to

his congregation that the views of the pulpit are his own point of view, in conscientiously endeavoring to reach the facts as he can see them, and that he is talking thus not because he happens to have been caught in the preacher's profession, but that he is a preacher because things seem to him to shape themselves in this way.

True preaching is founded on that strange unity in which the whole world of experience is bound together. Analogies seem to run through nature, human society and spiritual experience, in sensing these the preacher leads his congregation almost unconsciously into new realms in which the old familiar laws seem still to hold. The greatest examples of this experience are to be found in the parables of Jesus. But the old principle *operatio sequitur esse*, what you are determines the way you act, is never more pertinent as when you sit down to compose a sermon. The superficial mind starts on the surface and never gets inside his subject, the old soldier who has long ago dug himself into a complacent dogmatic rut contents himself with renewed splashing of the mud around, but the mind that is active and open and alert finds analogies presenting themselves from experience and reading on every hand. To live for one moment as Shakespeare lived, noticing and appreciating all the sounds and sights and colors and fragrances and comedies and tragedies and allusions and analogies of a single scene, to live for a moment even as a Sinclair Lewis does at his best, noting the oddness of the familiar, the quaintness of the contemporary, the folk lore of the present, the poetry and humor of common speech, the pinch of prosperity and the cosmic ironies of human life in a small town setting; to live for one moment as the saints have ever lived finding heroism and loyalty and devotion and divine beauty springing up around them everywhere and testifying that "all places which the eye of heaven visits are to the wise man ports and happy havens;" to live for one moment filled with the pity which Dante felt for those whose lives have become hopelessly tangled and awry:

Ah me! How many sweet thoughts and how much desire,
Conducted these unto this woful pass!

and to hear from even the most degraded and lost the cry that went forth from that sorrowful pair in Dante's Hell: "If the king of the universe were our friend!" [14] . . . it is out of moments like these that the inspiration for true preaching comes.

CHAPTER II

INSPIRATION

WITH your seed idea, your original inspiration in mind, you begin to try to express it. You have something valuable, something vital, something essential, to say. Immediately you discover that one of the most impassable roads in the world is that between the brain and the end of a pen. You think you know what you want to say, but how to make the end of a pen or a typewriter say it, that is the trick of style. The young minister who opened his prayer: "O God, in drawing near to thee, we pass from the seen to the unseen, from the tangible to the intangible, from the sphere of sense to the sphere of nonsense," did not say what he meant, or his words were too true to be wise. The whole problem of style is how to get your hearer or reader to see what you see, its outline, its colors, its movement, its meaning. As soon as we start to write down what we think we see in our own minds, we all inevitably do what we do in golf, we take our eyes off the ball, we write not what we see but what we have heard as usual phrases for describing such affairs. Anton Tchekov wrote to a friend who had sent him a story for his criticism: "Cut out all those pages about the moon-light, and give us instead what you feel about it—the reflection of the moon in a piece of broken bottle." Dostoevsky as quoted by Middleton Murry, in a similar case said to a writer who had described the throwing of pennies to an organ man in the street below, "I want to hear that penny hopping and chinking." [1] In order to convey an idea or impression to another it is necessary for you to hold it clearly in your own mind. When Wodehouse writes, "The door opened and the butler entered, a solemn procession of one," you see what he saw. Mr. Lascelles Abercrombie was staying at a cottage in England and asked the parson what kind of a flower a plant creeping over the cottage had when it was in bloom, the parson said, "Oh, it's an awfully jolly little flower!" But when he asked a ploughman, he said, "Oh, it's an innocent little blow." The parson answered without thinking much, the ploughman's mind seemed to linger lovingly over the picture of the flower in his mind as he answered. Compare the effect on your mind of the conventional description of scenery like this: "I do not think that I shall ever forget the sight of Etna at sunset: the mountain almost invisible in a blur of pastel gray, glowing on the top and then repeating its shape in a wisp of gray smoke, with the whole horizon behind radiant with pink light fading gently into a gray pastel sky," all of which probably means exactly nothing to hearer or reader, with a few words by Peter Fleming describing his entry into the port of Rio. The first thing he says which greets the visitor on the waterfront is a solitary skyscraper, out of place, forlorn, irrelevant, ridiculous, "It was," he says, "like a bag of tools left behind when the curtain rises on a stage set for romance."

Style is the art of getting people to see what you see. It is through contemplation or meditation that the writer of the sermon attains to that inner vision which sees clearly what he wants his hearers to see with him. The whole set of modern life is opposed to any exercise of this form of mental discipline. The pause between conception and execution seems to the modern world to be the interposition of an unnecessary vacuum. Yet it is in this period of incubation that the seed germ really comes to life. A more consistent observation of this period of meditation before the writing of the sermon would both enrich and correct the first impression of the truth, and save many a thoughtful spirit in the congregation from thinking with gentle irony what Socrates thought of Agathon: "Whereas my wisdom is meagre and dreamlike, yours is all splendor and promise." [2] It is in this period when you fix this vision of yours in the eye, look all around it, catch its various implications and connections, modify its scope, enlarge and deepen its foundations that the bones of the sermon are formed.

But in order to be reasonable you need something more than reason, nor is good will a sufficient equipment for a preacher. He must respect the medium in which he works and learn his art. One often learns more from those artists who work in a different medium from one's own. This period of meditation and reflexion before execution is to be found in all

the arts. Notice how Blake meditates upon the tiger,
on the brightness streaked with black, the bound, the
suppleness, the ferocity till his mind moves from idea
tiger to idea flame, and he writes the line: "Tiger,
tiger, burning bright." Hear what Rainer Maria Rilke
says of his observation of the methods of Rodin, the
sculptor: "He examines carefully. He is not satisfied
with his first impression or his second or many others.
He studies and notes. He makes sketches of move-
ments so trivial as to be inexpressible in words, gestures and half gestures, forty abbreviated notes, eighty
profiles. He surprises his model in habitual or in
chance attitudes, in ways of expressing himself which
are checked and suppressed, in poses of weariness and
intense excitement. He becomes familiar with all the
passing changes in his features, knows how a smile
starts and dies away. He lives in the man's face as in
a scene in which he himself takes part, he stands in
the centre of it and nothing that happens there is
indifferent to him or unobserved. He takes nothing
for granted, he will know nothing but what he sees.
But he sees everything." [3]

Nothing better has ever been written to describe
this period of meditation before execution, and what
is true of one art is true of all the arts. There is a
knack at the heart of every art which cannot fully be
described in words, and this power of holding an
idea in the mind and meditating upon it is one such
knack. It is not day dreaming, it is not consecutive
thinking as yet, it is analogous to the slow mastication
of a crust of bread, the catching the flavor, a curious

passiveness which is farthest removed from sluggish-
ness of mind, an openness to suggestion from all the
stored richness of experience, a feeling outward of the
tendrils of the mind for connections and support, an
alertness for new impressions. "Look, listen, but don't
move." One lets truth and beauty sink in as one does
standing before a wonderful scene, when one is not
sure what one does, but the eyes wander from this
part to the other and seem to be drinking in form and
color and composition with appreciation and delight.
The result is increased sensitiveness and the multiplica-
tion of associations or echoes. The analogy is perhaps
most perfect in the experience of listening to music
when appreciation, understanding, passivity, respon-
siveness, are all present, when one does not light like
a bird and then immediately fly off again, but one
considers the same theme from many points of view
with constantly enlarging understanding and pleasure.
The mind so started upon its way by such a period of
reflexion continues unconsciously to develop the
theme given to it. The delightful sequence of the third
Psalm is true in this connection as well as in conditions of despondency:

"Lord, how are they increased that trouble me!
many are they that rise up against me. . . . I laid me
down and slept; I awaked; for the Lord sustained me.
I will not be afraid of ten thousands of people, that
have set themselves against me round about." In the
morning after a good night's sleep the mind is often
found upon its own to have done wonders to the subject matter given to it the night before.

And so we come to the actual writing of the sermon. It is necessary not merely to visualize the message but to visualize the message being delivered to the congregation. Borrowing an illustration from Vernon Lee, the craft of preaching is the power of manipulating the contents of the hearer's mind. The preacher "has felt life in such a manner as to make it desirable that his feelings be communicated to others." The end of preaching is the response of the hearer to the suggestions of the preacher. The mind of the congregation is the preacher's palette. The preacher is really "playing upon the contents of the hearer's mind as the pianist is playing on the strings." [4]

Only on one occasion can the writer remember the publication of a sermon with footnotes as to the reaction of the congregation. One such footnote to a sermon preached by the rector of a New York church sticks in the memory, after one statement there was an asterisk, and at the bottom of the page this note, "Here a little girl near the front looked up at her mother as though to say 'How can the man say anything so ridiculous!' " Volumes of published sermons would probably pay better if such footnotes as to results and reactions became the rule rather than the exception. "A great effort!" remarked the deacon to the military man after the minister had at length sat down mopping his brow, and in Crothers' essay, the military man enquired, "An effort at what?" This habit of appending footnotes as to net gains due to the delivery of the sermon ought to be encouraged. After many an eloquent "effort" the note might be added, "net gain nil;" the writer remembers only a few recordable gains in thirty years. In one case a lawyer who said: "After your sermon I got the idea of a Communion service for the first time, and stayed for it, and it did a great deal for me." On another occasion a lumber merchant said: "On Monday after that sermon, I telephoned my advertising man to remove all bill boards of mine from public roads." And after a sermon on social justice a banker said: "It would have been all right if you had said it was only an ideal." Of course the results of preaching are in the nature of the case largely unknown. The people who liked the sermon come up sometimes and tell the preacher it was "the greatest sermon they ever heard," the people who think the sermon was below contempt generally go out saying nothing. So every minister's wife who is worth her salt reminds her husband when she notices signs of incipient self-satisfaction, but if she is wise she will repress her observation till at least Tuesday, the minister is entitled after his "effort" to gloat over the compliments at least till that day in the week. Some ministers place the offering after the sermon as a rough test of results, but as the value of the currency of the kingdom is in proportion to the unexpended balance (Mark 12:41-44), this method is hardly valid. As in firms of lawyers the individual lawyer's fee for a case goes "into the pot" for the advantage of all the members of the firm, so the good done by any sermon goes into the pot of merit acquired by all those who are working for righteousness, and becomes an indistinguishable part of the force of good will hidden like leaven in the somewhat sodden dough of human life. One of the disadvantages encountered by those who devote their lives to disinterested labor for the common good is that the public takes them at their word and treats them as if they really were disinterested.

It has been said that the difference between a good piece of writing and a good speech is that in the first case the thread on which the thought is strung is the reasoned argument, in the second case the thread is the personality of the speaker. This is a dangerous half truth, comforting to lazy minds. Congregations may believe it, but preachers should not pay any attention to it or should phrase it thus: "It is easier for a poor preacher than for a poor writer to keep those he is talking to awake, for the preacher can always thump the pulpit." But the radio is equipped with a blessed device which deprives the radio pulpit even of this small advantage. The congregation can turn the preacher off. There is, however, a distinction between a discourse which is designed to be read and one which is intended to be heard. In *Diana of the Crossways* we read of oratory that "It is always the more impressive for the spice of temper which renders it untrustworthy." [5] A learned professor recently stated that it was impossible to speak in public and tell the truth. If one were to guard and qualify each statement, as would be necessary to convey the exact truth, one's discourse, he said, would be so unutterably tedious that there would be no one to listen to it. But it must be noted that the man who said this was a professor,

who is a teacher rather than a preacher, and there is
a distinction. The academic teacher's job is to show
you how you walk, the preacher shows you how to
walk. The teacher cannot be satisfied till you understand the process of walking. The preacher is interested in getting you to walk. All preachers are teachers
to a certain extent and all teachers, especially those
who go out of their way to avoid being thought so,
are preachers, on the basis at least of the modified
Emersonian adage, "What you are preaches so loud
that I cannot hear what you teach!" But the jobs are
distinct jobs. The distinction between the slant of an
essay or treatise written to be read and a sermon or
speech written to be delivered orally is real but subtle.
The human animal is a more patient sufferer as a
reader than as a hearer, partly perhaps because he is
usually in a more comfortable position; even the
greatest short stories are generally edited and abbreviated when read in public. The intellectual age of most
congregations or audiences is less advanced than can
be counted on in a self-selected group of readers. You
can read a sentence twice, but the speaker goes on.
The speaker speaks to the eternal child. When Martineau was a small boy in the nursery his mother came
upon him reading the Bible, he informed her that he
was reading the whole Bible through, adding as she
reached the door, "skipping the nonsense, of course,
mamma." Much that is valuable in writing for readers
who select themselves, it is nonsense to address to a
miscellaneous audience. It is possible to be as deep as
you are capable of being, but you must be simple,

erudition has its effective uses but all pedantry is lost effort. The end of preaching is to inspire people how to live.

The last few years have seen a great revival in the belief in the confessional as opposed to public worship and preaching. It is said to be ridiculous to administer the same remedy to a crowd of people each of whom needs special treatment, as well might a doctor dose his patients en masse out of the same bottle, irrespective of their complaints. Each human being it is said, should consult an expert who will analyze him psychically and show him what exactly is wrong with him. It is a useful method, and has been proved so by generations of use in the Roman Catholic church, but its weak point is that the number of people who have such abundant sources of inner inspiration as to be normally balanced themselves, at all times and in all respects, is so few, that it sometimes seems as if it might be necessary to produce a group of superexperts to analyze these experts continually, and keep their lives magnificently wise and profoundly human, so that they may continually live at the heights necessary for their difficult work. The method is not enough unless it is in the hands of great artists in the art of living.

The implied criticism of preaching and public worship is hardly valid. The preacher as a preacher is not a consulting physician, however much of such work he may do at other times. His work is more comparable to the activity of a director of public health engaged in promoting the general health of the community. To raise the tone of the mental, moral and spiritual life of a community is an even more difficult task than that of performing a similar service for the people's physical life. In order to write an effective sermon the preacher must have his congregation in the back of his mind during the whole period of composition. The ideal sermon is addressed to a particular congregation. The power of much that is said is due to the fact that it is this particular man whom they know who is saying it. There are some common, one might almost say, plebeian virtues, graces and gifts, which are almost universally respected. They may not be the rarer and loftier achievements of human character. But they gain for the possessor the respect and affection of his fellows. If a man is known to be a good sport, to have a sense of humor, to be charitable and kind-hearted and broad-minded, and human enough to play a good game and enjoy ordinary pleasures, then when he does speak on spiritual themes his opinion has some weight with ordinary folks. He may have the gift of prophecy and understand all mysteries and all knowledge, and have all faith, and be ascetic and otherworldly, and have a private line to the Almighty, but if he gets mad when beaten at tennis, or leaves the lawn mower he has borrowed out all night in the rain, or does not pay his bills or keep his nails clean, all his otherworldly virtues profit him nothing with the average member of his congregation. If you possess some of these common understandable virtues you can add to them all the most mystical virtues of a more rarefied spiritual air, but in these times one must manifest an approved life in the outer court of common folk before one can be credited with having penetrated into the Holy of Holies. Nor should clergymen object to this rule of thumb by which they are judged as if it were class discrimination. Ordinary folk are apt to judge all human pretensions by the same yardstick. They like to hear or read about people who have done something worthy of note in a field which is comprehensible to them. While this habit of mind is often unfair to geniuses in their own day, it is not a bad way of judging ordinary men.

The minister writes his sermon as a man who is known, for a group he knows.

The ideal position for a professional man to occupy in any community is that of being liked and respected for his own sake as a human being, and at the same time trusted and depended upon for his expert professional knowledge and skill. It is very difficult for the minister in our days to attain to this position in his community. On the one hand he is apt to know men only professionally, in and through their relationship with the church. The relation of people to him is apt to become their relation to him as a minister. A minister took a job in a tinsmith's shop in order to practice his former trade, and earn some money towards the expenses of taking his doctorate. The shop was far away from his parish, and he was not known to be a minister. All went well. His relation with his fellow workmen was friendly and unconstrained. One day, however, a letter inadvertently arrived at the shop addressed to him as "Reverend." The truth came out. He said that in spite of all he could do, he could never reëstablish the same natural and intimate relations with his fellows again. They assumed unnatural poses in conversing with him, and sunk their voices when he arrived. A ship's companion with whom the writer had had many interesting conversations on the way over the Atlantic, many of them on religious matters, said to him, as the boat was coming in to Southampton: "The trouble with ministers is that of the very nature of the case it is impossible for us to talk to them as we have been talking, and so they never find out how we ordinary men feel about these things." This disadvantage is shared to a certain extent by all the professions, but it is more unfortunate in the case of the ministry. It is as unwise to attempt to escape from one's professional pedestal by adopting what one may consider the laxity of lay manners as it would be for a judge to loaf around the doors of his court gossiping with the lawyers and witnesses about the cases, or for a doctor with a cold to sneeze into people's faces because the public usually does so. A natural relationship with one's fellows can only be maintained when one works and plays with them. A minister must be more than a minister if he is to have sane views of the race of men, he must work with them and play with them in activities not directly connected with the church, he must be regarded by others as one of the men present, rather than primarily as a minister. So the picture of his congregation in the back of his mind as he composes, his sermon will be more lifelike.

If a minister is to have a self-respecting position in a community, there must also be respect for his knowledge and skill in the particular field in which he is an expert. St. Francis of Sales said: "The knowledge of the priest is the eighth sacrament of the church." Thus arises the most difficult question: What is the particular field in which the minister is an expert? The truth is that under modern conditions some ministers tend to become just good fellows around town. The days when they were the only highly educated persons, when they alone knew the sacred books in their original tongues, are gone. It may have been impossible to save Hebrew, but it was probably a mistake to let Greek go. One man in any community who enjoyed reading Homer and Plato and the New Testament in the original might have more to give from a spiritual point of view than three men who had spent the precious hours in Theological School over the statistics of Philanthropy, the variables of Economics, or the platitudes of Education. But for the present the study of the sacred texts in their original languages has been crowded out of most theological curricula, and in what now is the minister an expert? We can say that he ought to be an expert in religion. All human wisdom seems to be the flesh that clothes certain bones, the crystallization which collects in a saturated solution around something hard and firm. The original languages of the sacred texts were for centuries the hard difficult core round which spiritual wisdom gathered. They served as the test and exercise for minds worthy of becoming leaders in such matters. On these disciplines the mind cut its teeth, they gave the mind something tangible to chew upon. They forced the mind to exert itself in an efficient and orderly manner. The King James version of the Bible may have been in many cases more inspired than the original documents, but it was to minds which had been disciplined on those original documents that the inspiration came. The minister today feels himself too much of an amateur in that field which like education is a paradise for amateurs, religion. He can no longer cow the layman with a reference to the original text. Religion in itself is such an evanescent and debatable field that to claim to be an expert in it savors of the faker. Yet it is fatal to descend to lower levels, and only claim to be an expert orator, or teller of stories to children, or organizer of women's societies, or enlister of Sunday School teachers, or money raiser. A minister if not an expert on religion is nothing much: "Religion in its decay sinks back into sociability." [6] Yet the word "religion" does not seem to consort very well with the word "expert." This is partly because of the historical identification of so much of religion with passivity or at most childlike acceptance. St. Paul was careless in not using more footnotes. Many times he let his letters go out unasterisked, when he ought occasionally to have added notes to some of his pronouncements to the effect: "This is the way I feel this morning!" or "This is the mood I am in now!" He did not realize that future œcumenical councils, obsessed by mechanical views of inspiration, would insist on either killing or being killed in defence of the absolute and final truth of their interpretations of every chance remark he made.

Father Vann notes that "Some philosophers forget that there is an art of being a philosopher," [7] and St. Paul would have agreed in some of his moods that there is an art of being religious. To be religious is to attain to a certain attitude of mind and activity, a special way of living, bringing one within the sphere of action of certain beneficent laws or principles which run through all life. To achieve this power, one has to learn to control the mind and imagination in a specific manner. The Gulf Stream will flow through a straw if it is turned in the right direction, but there is an art in finding the Stream, and keeping the straw of one's life directed in the correct way. The life of prayer, as opposed to the life of worry, is the best example of what is meant. At the limits of human endeavor there is always an overflow of desire. This overflow may either run amok into worry, or be organized into the life of prayer. There is an art in so organizing it, for we live in an orderly world; there is great difficulty in doing so, as we all know. The religious leader must be one who has given much time and thought and endeavor to learning from the saints, and experimenting with methods for so directing the mind and indeed the whole being. The teachings of the Bible alternately emphasize the ease and the difficulty of this process. There is the picture of the little child in the midst, of the yoke that is easy and the burden that is light, but there is also the picture of one's taking up one's cross and following, of the strait and narrow way which few find. Like every art it is desperately hard, almost impossible to learn; like every art, when achieved it seems simplicity itself. The ease and pleasure with which Romney paints his pictures of children, the way in which Kreisler simply takes up his violin and draws the bow across it do not deceive us into thinking that it was easy work learning to do these things, and the art of religion manifested in faith, serenity, courage, self-control, mercy, inspiration, character, is at least no easier than the other arts. Underneath the surface manifestations, applauded by men, there is a whole inner world of discipline, practice, persistence, failure, labor and agony of spirit.

In the famous Whistler trial the Attorney-General asked about the *Nocturne in Black and Gold* which Whistler said it had taken him two days to paint: "The labour of two days, then, is that for which you ask two hundred guineas?" Whistler answered: "No; I ask it for the knowledge of a lifetime." After Whistler's death Mr. Walter Gay wrote about his early struggles: "No one can realize, who has not watched Whistler paint, the agony that his work gave him. I have seen him, after a day's struggle with a picture, when things did not go, completely collapse, as from an illness. His drawing cost him infinite trouble. I have known him work two weeks on a hand, and then give it up discouraged." [8] It is on that "knowledge of a lifetime" in the personal experience of religion that even the youngest minister must depend as he sits down to compose his sermon. Much as he would dislike being called an expert, it must be on the basis of his own inner struggle to come to the experience of the religious life that he has any right to lead others. There is such a condition as holiness, much as the massive grandeur of the word scares us today. John Wesley said: "How hard it is to be shallow enough for a polite audience!" And it is probably unwise to talk much of the deeper experiences. But to have some experience of them is an aim worth the trial.

The great preacher always gives the impression of speaking only a little of what he knows. His message has an unspoken background which gives it depth and substance. His whole bearing is that of one who is only showing you some of his treasures, "I have yet many things to say unto you, but ye cannot bear them now." There is no greater benefit that a man can confer on his fellows than his own achievement of some measure of personal holiness,[9] some experience of the discipline, organization and intensification of his own inner life. Certain phrases seem to indicate better than detailed descriptions could do specimen religious attitudes of resignation, courage, need, irony, faith, etc., of which the preacher must have had some personal experience in his own life, as, "The Practice of the Presence of God," "The Expulsive Power of a New Affection," "I cannot do otherwise, Here I stand, God help me," "I am in earnest—I will not equivocate—I will not excuse—I will not retreat a single inch—and I will be heard," "So long Thy power hath led us, sure

it still will lead us on," "I would fain be to the Eternal
Goodness, what his own hand is to a man," "In His
will is our peace," "The law in its majestic equality
forbids the rich as well as the poor to sleep under
bridges, to beg in the streets and to steal bread," "O
wretched man that I am! who shall deliver me from
the body of this death?"

But one touch of insincerity can put an entire sermon off key. Even in small matters it is better to be
content with a natural blunt point rather than by an
insincere effort to make it unnaturally sharp. Few people imagine how closely they are watched by others
in this matter. How surprised Guizot would be to read
in an account given of him by one who knew him
well: "The knowledge which he had gained in the
morning, he repeated in the afternoon with the air of
a man who had known it from all eternity." [10] It is
extraordinary how one comes to trust a man given to
understatement.

"An expert in the practice of religion"—it is a hate-
ful way of expressing something which he must be;
in addition he must be an artist in his ability to com-
municate lofty moods of being. "The great instrument of moral good is the imagination," said Shelley.
The preacher must learn the use of this instrument
from the masters. The greatest teaching is never direct. You learn something best from someone who is
not thinking of teaching you that thing. You can
learn most about the use of the great instrument of
moral improvement not from other preachers but from
artists, poets, musicians. The minister's reading should

be in the great classic writers of imaginative literature. For the simple pious soul they do not seem to be very useful because they do not go far enough or do not preach clearly enough. But for the minister they are the great teachers, because they possess the supreme art of conveying to others the loftiest moods. A play like *King Lear* should only be less dear to him than his Bible, while it does not say the things he has to say, it conveys the mood in which his message must be delivered if it is to reach the inner selves of those to whom he preaches. Dr. J. Dover Wilson says: "In *King Lear* Shakespeare succeeded in showing Truth, at its bleakest and most terrifying, as Beauty; in *The Tempest* he succeeded in showing Beauty, at its serenest, most magical and most blessed, as Truth." [11] To be able to speak what the preacher feels about God and immortality, not abstractly or even theologically, but with the same power of elevating the spirit in grandeur and magnificence, that should be the far distant aim of every preacher. Why should not something of the same magic which Wordsworth makes the reader feel about the valley of the Wye creep into the preacher's sermon about the love of God or the loveliness of virtue?

> These beauteous Forms,
> Through a long absence, have not been to me
> As is a landscape to a blind man's eye:
> But oft, in lonely rooms, and 'mid the din
> Of towns and cities, I have owed to them,
> In hours of weariness, sensations sweet,
> Felt in the blood, and felt along the heart;

And passing even into my purer mind,
With tranquil restoration: — — — Nor less, I trust,
To them I may have owed another gift,
Of aspect more sublime; that blessed mood,
In which the burthen of the mystery,
In which the heavy and the weary weight
Of all this unintelligible world,
Is lightened:—that serene and blessed mood,
In which the affections gently lead us on,—
Until, the breath of this corporeal frame
And even the motion of our human blood
Almost suspended, we are laid asleep
In body, and become a living soul:
While with an eye made quiet by the power
Of harmony, and the deep power of joy,
We see into the life of things.[12]

The fact that even Wordsworth's genius failed him
when he tried to write ecclesiastical sonnets should
not wholly discourage the preacher of today from an
attempt to speak of spiritual things with the same art
as the poets have used in speaking of earthly things.
After all, the message of today lends itself more to
this inspired expression than did the cast-iron logical
systems of the past, and there is an encouraging parable in the sixteenth chapter of Luke in which a certain steward seems to be strangely commended for
learning from other arts than his own, "for the children of this world are in their generation wiser than
the children of light."

As a man whom his congregation knows, and as one
in whose knowledge of his subject they have some

confidence, the minister sits down to compose his sermon. His views upon things are, under these circumstances, not exactly what they believe to be their
views. How should he go about to bring them to think
a little more as he thinks? This is indeed a problem.
The minister must respect his congregation, remembering Dr. Johnson's penetrating words of charity
when Boswell told him that Dr. John Campbell drank
thirteen bottles of port at a sitting, and Johnson said:
"However, I loved Campbell: he was a solid orthodox
man; he had a reverence for religion. Though defec-
tive in practice, he was religious in principle." [13] It is
clear that mere scolding is out of place in the pulpit.
Under a rain of denunciation most modern hearers
put up their umbrellas and let the drips run on to
their neighbors' shoulders. It is better to lead the congregation along, starting with certain general principles to which they gladly assent and then applying
these to unexpected special instances, and modestly
inferring how is it possible to escape the obvious ap-
plications. It is not a question of cowardice or courage,
it is a question of method. Dr. John Tillotson, afterwards Archbishop of Canterbury, preached a sermon
upon the Golden Rule in 1660. In it he says: "It is
to be fear'd, that something very like Unrighteousness
is woven into the Mysterys of most Trades; and like
Phidias's Image in Minerva's Shield, cannot be de-
fac'd without the Ruin of it. I think this is not a
groundless Jealousy, but the Confession and Complaint of the most knowing and understanding Persons in most Human Affairs: I shall instance only in

the slightness of Work, the imbasing of Commoditys, and setting them off by indirect Advantages. I can only bewail this; for unless the World could generally be convinc'd of this, it is not like to be amended. Perfection is not to be look'd for in this imperfect State, we must be content if things are passable." [14] This is perhaps too true to be homiletical, one can at least understand why Whitefield saw in this preacher the conspicuous representative of the lukewarmness of the religion of the time, and why Voltaire called him the wisest and most eloquent of English preachers.

The modern reader is inclined to think that there is a more self-respecting position, likely to be more efficacious, between this uneasy acquiescence in things as they are and John the Baptist's "Generation of Vipers." It is wisdom on the part of a speaker to be very generous in the recognition of the difficulties which lie in the way of his own solution of the problem he is discussing. Jesus certainly did not minimize obstacles. One ancient Greek medical philosopher appended to his theory a note which began with these words: "My opponent's view will be assisted by the following considerations." [15] More good may be done by a sermon on War and Peace if the speaker does not assume that continents which have for centuries been immersed up to the neck in the middle of an endless treacherous and slimy bog could, if they really wanted to, leave it by a four-way concrete boulevard. M. Elie Faure will gain more sober assent when he speaks thus of war: "Man is above all an artist. He only rejects those forms of art that are exhausted. The desire of perpetual peace will not kill this form of art unless the conditions of peace involve a new method of warfare, with the same sudden and collective intoxication, the same shining responsibilities, the same creative risks, the same atmosphere of voluntarily accepted tragedy." A frontal attack on the wage scale in the steel industry is likely to have little effect when delivered to a congregation of steel manufacturers, the preacher may feel he is saving his own soul, but it is to be feared that other souls will not be saved during the sermon. The attitude of the congregation will probably be similar to that of the poor family who met the charity visitor at the door of their house with the remark: "You get outer here, ye can't save your soul off of us!" There is the old difficulty which always arises between the popularizer and the specialist.

A recent perfect example is to be seen in Dr. James H. Breasted's review of the first volume of Will Durant's *The Story of Civilization* in *The Saturday Review of Literature* for July 13, 1935, with its delightful sentence, which might almost have been written by one of the more polite of the steel manufacturers after the sermon mentioned above: "Under these circumstances I have found the writing of this review a very ungracious and unwelcome task; for it is not a little distressing to criticize thus the work of a writer of unusual literary gifts who has, seemingly all unawares, involved himself in such insuperable difficulties." Even the youngest minister cannot hope to know as much about the Steel business as those men who have spent their lives in it. In many such matters he must be a popularizer of popularizers. Should he therefore be silent in the face of what he may believe to be a manifest injustice? He cannot be silent. He must do everything he can do to change a condition he believes to be iniquitous. The words of Chrysostom about the "kept parson," the "trencher chaplain," will ring in the burning ears of the popular minister: "Rich men keep these lecturers, and fawning parasites, like so many dogs at their tables, and filling their hungry guts with the offal of their meat, they abuse them at their pleasure, and make them say what they propose." It is reported that God once asked the Devil this riddle: "Which will do the more harm, a good man who is part of a bad machine, or a bad man who is part of a good machine?" The Devil who had been reading the New Testament replied, "The good man went away sorrowful, but still rich and active. The bad man hanged himself. By which, I suppose, is meant that the machine is too strong for the man. Let me organize society, and you can send all the good men you want into it." But God said: "The machine is made by men." The preacher, hearkening to this parable, cannot refuse to do his bit to reorganize the social and economic machine, as parts of which the individual young people of his parish have to take their places in life.

But he must remember that he is speaking to men who are caught in a system just as truly as he himself is caught in the same system. He must read Bernard Shaw's *Major Barbara*. "He must either share the world's guilt or go to another planet." [16] When Father John Neville Figgis was lecturing at Cambridge some years ago, he paused in one of his lectures to make a personal confession, which ran something like this: "Here am I who seem to have done everything a man can do to disassociate myself from the system. I have given up everything I possessed, I do not own even the clothes I wear, they belong to the order of which I am a member. And yet I have not been able to get out of it. These clothes are ultimately paid for, the cell I live in is provided for me out of the profits of the same system from which I tried to escape." As a fellow struggler, rather than as one who possesses loftier ideals than theirs, the preacher can do more to change what he believes to be an unjust system. If you believe that nothing less than a bloody revolution can change things for the better, the soap box will be your pulpit, where you will talk no longer to those who have at present power and influence in the matter: and your theme will be "Revolution Without Tarrying for Any." And there is a great work to be done in undermining the patience of the poor. But if you still have faith in the good streaks to be found in all human nature, you may elect to stay in the pulpit and see what can be done by a more gradual and bloodless revolution. If so, you will not disdain to use wise tactics. You will try and find something in these matters on which you and your congregation can agree, and be making frequent sallies out into the debatable land just beyond their last line of trenches. Perhaps some of them will follow you a little way.

At any rate they will not be as hopeless as they might have been if they did not have to listen to you once in a while. It is your chance to give them the other side of the arguments they hear everywhere else. As one deacon said: "I cannot follow my minister in all that he says, but I like my minister to be a little ahead of me." All this depends upon your being able to persuade them that you are more than a mere theoretical revolutionist. Most heretics have been burned not entirely because they were heretics, but because they were also unpleasant persons. Scotland some years ago put one great scholar out of the church because they could not see anything in him but his radical views, but when a younger scholar of the same name and similar views appeared, they were afraid to excommunicate him because of the great work he was doing for the youth of their land. The parents of the boys whom he had literally saved from hell, would have risen up and in the name of humanity excommunicated the church, had they tried to do so. As has been indicated before, you can get away with much of the gospel even in the modern church, if you are humanly and religiously as well as socially minded. You can be as unpleasant a person as you like if you are sure you are a genius, but of that you cannot be sure till you have made a study of the books written a hundred years after your death. You can be as unpleasant a person as you please if you are willing to take the consequences, and the world needs such if life is to be kept from becoming a sickly syrup, but the unfortunate people are those who feel it their duty to be unpleasant, and yet angrily protest at the injustice of the treatment they receive. The world needs both kinds of people, Luther and Erasmus, though neither will ever much admire the other and it will be still many years before we can finally make up our minds which of them really did the most for the human race. Perhaps it would take more courage today to live and die like Sir Thomas More than to follow the belligerent stride of Luther or the tactful gait of Erasmus. It was More who dared to say that what we call government is but "a conspiracy of the rich seeking their own commodity under the name of the common weal," it was More who taught us how a non-conformist unjustly condemned to the scaffold can die: "On the way to the Tower, his daughter Meg was on the wharf, and as she saw him land, she ran through the guard that with halberts and bills were round him, 'and took him about the neck and kissed him.' Next day, with a coal, he wrote her the hour of his execution. It was to be St. Thomas's eve, 'a day very meet and convenient for me. And I never liked your manners better, than when you kissed me last. For I like when daughterly love and dear charity hath no leisure to look to worldly courtesy.' As the messenger, Sir Thomas Pope, broke into tears, before he took him to the place of execution, he comforted him. 'Quiet yourself, good Mr. Pope, and be not discomforted. For I trust that we shall once in heaven see each other full merrily.' " [17] It is great to suffer for one's faith. It is divine to be able to do so in that debonair spirit of good cheer. He was a Roman Catholic who was hard on Protestants, and yet in life and death may be numbered among the greatest of English non-conformists. If the preacher is called upon to suffer for his faith, if he can do no otherwise than testify on the unpopular side, let him learn courage from Luther, wisdom from Erasmus and courtesy from Sir Thomas More!

CHAPTER III

THE CHURCH-GOING TRADITION IN ENGLISH LITERATURE

BUT we take it that the particular sermon we are discussing is not to be a world-shaking pronouncement, but rather a humble attempt to place before his congregation some freshly experienced truth of the religious life. He has been trying to orientate himself before he sits down to write out the inspiration over which he has been meditating. Now he sits down to write.

The course of these lectures reminds one of the action in a certain famous Russian novel, in which the reader finds the hero on the first page in bed thinking of getting up, one is well through the book before the hero has got so far as to put one toe gingerly out of the bedclothes in the direction of the floor. One's only excuse is that fewer bad sermons would be preached if more went on in the minister's mind while they were being composed.

But before he actually begins to write, it is fitting that he should indulge in a short reverie, appreciating this strange custom of going to church, which provides him with his audience. Like a gold thread of poetry it has woven itself especially into the national life of the English-speaking peoples. As a mere habit, it is undoubtedly losing its place at the present time, crowded out by the more variegated pattern of modern life, except where real preaching appeals to the minds and hearts of individuals, or mystic ceremony fills the multitude with hereditary awe and troubles their minds with thoughts beyond the reaches of their souls.

Someone should edit a "Going to Church Anthology." It would open with Psalm 122, sung by the choir of a Scotch Presbyterian Church without instrumental accompaniment to the tune "St. Paul", in that doggerel metre so dear to those for whom it was the earliest music and poetry:

> I joyed when to the house of God,
>   Go up, they said to me.
> Jerusalem, within thy gates
>   Our feet shall standing be.
> Jerusalem, as a city, is
>   Compactly built together:
> Unto that place the tribes go up,
>   The tribes of God go thither.

The clergy of English literature! Could one gather together anywhere such a colorful group of worthies! Chaucer's "Povre Persoun of a town," who gave his parishioners this ensample, "That first he wroughte, and afterwards he taughte," and did not leave his sheep "encombred in the myre, And ran to London, un-to seynt Poules, To seken him a chaunterie for soules," "But Cristes lore, and his apostles twelve, He taughte, but first he folwed it him-selve." This poor parson had with him his brother, a ploughman, "That hadde y-lad of dong ful many a fother," such was the democracy of the church in Chaucer's days. Mr. Fielding's Parson Adams is another of those characters beside whose robust reality we living people seem to be but shades, Parson Adams who knew what it was to be unjustly treated so that "I remained, sir, a considerable time without any cure, and lived a full month on one funeral sermon, which I preached on the indisposition of a clergyman," Parson Adams who when restored to service was politic enough to be able to hold his position because, as he said, "On all proper seasons, such as the approach of an election, I throw a suitable dash or two into my sermons; which I have the pleasure to hear is not disagreeable to Sir Thomas and the other honest gentlemen my neighbors, who have all promised me these five years to procure an ordination for a son of mine, who is now near thirty, hath an infinite stock of learning, and is, I thank Heaven, of an unexceptionable life." [1] Addison has given us in the picture of Sir Roger de Coverley's church and minister, a scene which refreshes, as with a cup of pure spring water, lips dry with sophisticated dust. Sir Roger tells us how he had chosen his minister, "That he was afraid of being insulted with *Latin* and *Greek* at his own table; for which reason he desired a particular friend of his at the University to find him out a clergyman rather of plain sense than much learning, of a good aspect, a clear voice, a sociable temper, and, if possible a man that understood a little of back-gammon. My friend found me out this gentleman, who, besides the endowments required of him, is they tell me, a good scholar, tho' he does not shew it. . . . At his first settling with me, I made him a present of all the good sermons which have been printed in *English*, and only begged of him that every *Sunday* he would pronounce one of them in the pulpit. Accordingly, he has digested them into such a series, that they follow one another naturally, and make a continued system of practical divinity." "I am always very well pleased with a country Sunday," the Spectator continues, "and think, if keeping holy the seventh day were only a human institution, it would be the best way that could have been thought of for the polishing and civilizing of mankind. It is certain the country people would soon degenerate into a kind of savages and barbarians, were there not such frequent returns of a stated time, in which the whole village meet together with their best faces, and in their cleanliest habits, to converse with one another upon indifferent subjects, hear their duties explained to them, and join together in adoration of the Supreme Being. *Sunday* clears away the rust of the whole week. . . . As Sir Roger is landlord to the whole congregation, he keeps them in very good order, and will suffer nobody to sleep in it besides himself; for if by chance he has been surprised into a short nap at sermon, upon recovering out of it he stands up and looks about him, and if he sees anybody else nodding, either wakes them himself, or sends his servants to them. . . . I was yesterday very much surprised to hear my old friend, in the midst of the service, calling out to one *John Matthews* to mind what he was about, and not disturb the congregation. This *John Matthews* it seems is remarkable for being an idle fellow, and at that time was kicking his heels for his diversion." [2]

This fair picture is compared by the Spectator with the terrible conditions in a neighboring village where the parson and the squire live in a perpetual state of war, so that the squire never comes to church, and the parson has threatened that "if he does not mend his manners, he will pray for him in the face of the whole congregation," where the villagers are becoming sceptics, for they are hardly ever "brought to regard any truth, that is preached to them, when they know there are several men of five hundred a year who do not believe it." What a different personality speaks of Sunday services fifty years later in Wesley's *Journal:* "I took my horse at half an hour past three. There was no moon, or stars, but a thick mist; so that I could see neither road, nor anything else; but I went as right as if it had been noon-day. When I drew nigh Pennruddock Moor, the mist vanished, the stars appeared, and the morning dawned; so I imagined all the danger was past; but when I was on the middle of the moor, the mist fell again on every side, and I quickly lost my way. I lifted up my heart. Immediately it cleared up, and I soon recovered the high-road. On Alstone Moor I missed my way again; and what, I believe, no stranger has done lately, rode through all the bogs, without any stop, till I came to the vale, and thence

to Hinely Hill. A large congregation met in the evening. I expounded part of the twentieth chapter of
the Revelation. But O what a time was this! It was as
though we were already standing before the 'great
white throne.' God was no less present with us in
prayer; when one just by me cried out with a loud
bitter cry. I besought God to give us a token that all
things should work together for good. He did so: he
wrote pardon upon her heart; and we all rejoiced unto
him with reverence. . . . I wonder at those who still
talk so loud of the indecency of field-preaching. The
highest indecency is in St. Paul's Church, where a
considerable part of the congregation are asleep, or
talking, or looking about, not minding a word the
preacher says. On the other hand, there is the highest
decency in a churchyard or field, when the whole
congregation behave and look as if they saw the Judge
of all, and heard Him speaking from heaven." [3]

What a picture of a sermon we have too in Myers'
Saint Paul, one might imagine it as a description of the
very experience of which Wesley was speaking in
this passage from his *Journal:*

Oft when the Word is on me to deliver
  Lifts the illusion and the truth lies bare;
Desert or throng, the city or the river,
  Melts in a lucid Paradise of air,—

Only like souls I see the folk thereunder,
  Bound who should conquer, slaves who should be
    kings,—

Hearing their one hope with an empty wonder,
  Sadly contented in a show of things;—

Then with a rush the intolerable craving
  Shivers throughout me like a trumpet-call,—
Oh to save these! to perish for their saving,
  Die for their life, be offered for them all! [4]

The harbor peace, the human and divine companionship of church-going, as felt by one who has known the awful loneliness of the sea breathes through Coleridge's conclusion of *The Ancient Mariner:*

> O sweeter than the marriage feast,
> 'Tis sweeter far to me,
> To walk together to the kirk
> With a goodly company!—
>
> To walk together to the kirk,
> And all together pray,
> While each to his great Father bends,
> Old men, and babes, and loving friends,
> And youths and maidens gay!
>
> Farewell, farewell! but this I tell
> To thee, thou Wedding-guest!
> He prayeth well, who loveth well
> Both man and bird and beast.
>
> He prayeth best, who loveth best
> All things both great and small;
> For the dear God who loveth us,
> He made and loveth all.

We find a similar tenderness in "The Village Black-smith" by Longfellow and in the poem "Vo'k a-comen into Church" in William Barnes' volume of poems in the Dorsetshire dialect, and in the character of Mrs. Deland's Dr. Lavender. One of the great church scenes in English fiction is in Thackeray's *Esmond:* when, after the long parting and misunderstanding, his mistress tells him of her experience in church that day: "And today, Henry, in the anthem, when they sang it, 'When the Lord turned the captivity of Zion, we were like them that dream,' I thought, yes, like them that dream—them that dream. And then it went, 'They that sow in tears shall reap in joy; and he that goeth forth and weepeth, shall doubtless come again with rejoicing, bringing his sheaves with him;' I looked up from the book, and saw you. I was not surprised when I saw you. I knew you would come, my dear, and saw the gold sunshine round your head." [5] One would have to include in the anthology such a poem as Kipling's "Eddi's Service" from *Rewards and Fairies*, which tells of a Christmas service on a stormy night at a chapel in the marshes, when none of the Saxons came, and the only audience was an old marsh donkey and a yoke-weary bullock, to whom just as if they were bishops, Eddi preached the Word. Only when the morning light came did his strange audience turn and gallop back to the marsh again. But the mockery of the Saxons did not move the priest, since he knew that no power on earth could close the house of God to those who wished to come to its services. [6]

In the section devoted to more formal and ritualistic

church services there would be much of Sir Walter
Scott who delighted in such descriptions:

> And slow up the dim aisle afar,
> With sable cowl and scapular,
> And snow-white stoles, in order due,
> The holy fathers, two and two,
> In long procession came;
> Taper, and Host, and book they bare,
> And holy banner, flourished fair
> With the Redeemer's name.
> Then mass was sung, and prayers were said,
> And solemn requiem for the dead;
> And bells tolled out their mighty peal
> For the departed spirit's weal;
> And ever in the office close
> The hymn of intercession rose;
> And far the echoing aisles prolong
> The awful burthen of the song,—
>> *Dies irae, dies illa,*
>> *Solvet saeclum in favilla.*[7]

In "Benedictio Domini" Ernest Dowson has caught
the atmosphere of Catholic devotion and peace:

Without, the sullen noises of the street!
    The voice of London, inarticulate,
Hoarse and blaspheming, surges in to meet
    The silent blessing of the Immaculate.

Dark is the church, and dim the worshippers,
    Hushed with bowed heads as though by some old spell,
While through the incense-laden air there stirs
    The admonition of a silver bell.

Dark is the church, save where the altar stands,
   Dressed like a bride, illustrious with light,
Where one old priest exalts with tremulous hands
   The one true solace of man's fallen plight.

Strange silence here: without, the sounding street
   Heralds the world's swift passage to the fire:
O Benediction, perfect and complete!
   When shall men cease to suffer and desire.[8]

Wordsworth's two sonnets "Inside of King's College Chapel, Cambridge," convey a similar sense of the consecration of an ecclesiastical interior, and Browning has in his poem "Christmas Eve" expressed his dissatisfaction both with the Dissenter and the Catholic as they comport themselves in church:

       I sent my elbow spikewise
At the shutting door, and entered likewise,
Received the hinge's accustomed greeting,
And crossed the threshold's magic pentacle,
And found myself in full conventicle,
—To wit, in Zion Chapel Meeting,
Of the Christmas-Eve of 'Forty-nine,
Which, calling its flock to their special clover,
Found all assembled and one sheep over,
Whose lot, as the weather pleased, was mine.
I had very soon enough of it.
The hot smell and the human noises,
And my neighbor's coat, the greasy cuff of it,
Were a pebble-stone that a child's hand poises,
Compared with the pig-of-lead-like pressure
Of the preaching man's immense stupidity,

> As he poured his doctrine forth, full measure,
> To meet his audience's avidity.[9]

Yet the poet also found himself hopelessly outside the door of the great cathedral service where:

> At the silver bell's shrill tinkling,
> Quick cold drops of terror sprinkling
> On the sudden pavement strewed
> With faces of the multitude.
> Earth breaks up, time flows away,
> In flows heaven, with its new day
> Of Endless life.

The mystic grandeur of the experience of one who has entered that door and made himself a part of the kneeling congregation has never been better expressed than by Dean Paget in his magnificently written essay on the Sacraments in *Lux Mundi*, by the sacraments, men "are to escape from all daily pettiness, all morbid self-interest, all preposterous conviction of their own importance, into a fellowship which spans all ages and all lands." [10] One of the most moving descriptions of divine service is in the twenty-third chapter of Walter Pater's *Marius the Epicurean*, "and so it came to pass that on this morning Marius saw for the first time the wonderful spectacle—of those who believe."

The section of humorous and serious criticism of preachers and church-going would afford much sport and concern both for editor and reader. Here one would find the Reverend Mr. Chadband, enquiring of his friends in a spirit of love as to the nature of "treuth," [11] here would be the awful description of the emptiness of mere ritual in that account of a service in Tolstoy's *Resurrection*,[12] here would be the transcript of that terrible hell-fire sermon preached to boys in James Joyce's *A Portrait of the Artist as a Young Man*, and the very caustic take-off of war sermons and "collection" sermons in Aldous Huxley's *Crome Yellow:* "Higher Criticism has made the war possible." And in the sermon for a collection for a War Memorial: "Those who had lost relations in the war might reasonably be expected to subscribe a sum equal to that which they would have had to pay in funeral expenses if the relative had died while at home. Further delay was disastrous!" [13]

Edith Sichel's picture of "the Athanasian Creed sung in the highest of spirits in a prosperous church filled with sealskin-jacketed mamas and blowsy old gentlemen" should have a place as well as her conclusion of the whole matter of sermons: "All the clergymen in the world cannot make one disbelieve in God." [14]

The novels of the Victorian era, as in Mrs. Oliphant and Mark Rutherford, are filled with accounts of sermons and services in parish churches and chapels.[15] In no country and in no period does the church-going tradition play so great a part in the life of a people. As soon as the masses of people ceased to fight about religion and began to fight about politics, this interest in sermons and church-going began to fade out of the popular books, though we still have in a writer like Mary Cholmondley a delightful description of a sermon in a parish church as recounted by two hearers, first by the Reverend James Gresley's adoring wife: "James is simply surpassing himself. 'Worms!' What a splendid comparison. The Churchman the full-grown man after the stature of Christ, and the Dissenter invertebrate like a worm cleaving to the earth. But possibly God in his mercy may let them slip in by a back door to heaven! How like him to say that, so generous, so wide-minded, taking the hopeful view of everything. How noble he looks. These are days in which we should stick to our colours. I wonder how he can think of such beautiful things." The other account of the same sermon is by the minister's more discriminating sister: "Dear James! How good he is; how much in earnest. But worms don't go in at back doors. Why are not clergymen taught a few elementary rules of composition before they are ordained? But perhaps no one will notice it except myself. James is certainly a saint. He has the courage of his opinions. I believe he loves God and the Church with his whole heart and would go to the stake for them, or would send me there if he thought it was for the good of my soul." [16]

The novels of William Dean Howells contain some fine sermons like that scene and congregation so feelingly described when Mr. Peck preached a sermon too radical for the local capitalist Mr. Gerrish, who rose in the midst of it and pulling up his children, some of whom had been asleep, one by one, urged them from behind, down the aisle and out of the church, so that, even in sleep, they might not be contaminated by such words as these: "Patriotism has been the virtue which

has secured an image of brotherhood, rude and imperfect, to large numbers of men within certain limits,
but nationality must perish before the universal ideal
of fraternity is realized. Charity is the holiest of the
agencies which have hitherto wrought to redeem the
race from savagery and despair; but there is something
holier yet than charity—and that is justice—the instinct
of righteous shame which . . . stirs in every honest
man's heart when his superfluity is confronted with
another's destitution, and which is destined to increase
in power till it becomes the social as well as the individual conscience. In the labor organizations which
have their bad side, I see evidence that the poor have
at last had pity on the poor, and will no more betray
and underbid and desert one another." [17]

In Harriet Beecher Stowe's stories there are many
church scenes and some sermons. No preacher can
read without a twinge of conscience the experience of
Dr. Cushing after his learned sermon upon the unim-
portance of Christmas, "If it had been important for
us to keep Christmas, certainly the date would not
have been left in uncertainty," and Clemens Alex-
andrinus "writing at the close of the second century,
speaks of the date of Christ's birth as an unimportant
and unsettled point," "when the audience broke up
and the doctor came down from the pulpit, he was
congratulated on his sermon as a masterpiece. Indeed
he had the success that a man has always when he
proves to an audience that they are in the right in
their previous opinions." [18]

Many such comments on preaching would fill the

humorous section of the anthology, as for instance the remark made by the butler at Litchfield Palace who when asked how Master James Lonsdale was getting on, replied: "He offends the people by reproving them for drunkenness. 'E should 'a stuck to the doctrine, sir, that could do no 'arm!" [19]

In what section should we place that scene in the whalers' church in New Bedford, when Father Mapple halted for an instant at the foot of the perpendicular rope ladder leading up to his pulpit, "cast a look upward, and then with a truly sailor-like but still reverential dexterity, hand over hand, mounted the steps as if ascending the main-top of his vessel—and after gaining the height, slowly turned round, and stooping over the pulpit, deliberately dragged up the ladder step by step, till the whole was deposited within, leaving him impregnable in his little Quebec," thus signifying "his spiritual withdrawal for the time, from all outward worldly ties and connections." "What could be more full of meaning?" adds Melville, "for the pulpit is ever this world's foremost part. The pulpit leads the world. Yes, the world's a ship on its passage out, and not a voyage complete; and the pulpit is its prow"? [20]

Mr. T. S. Eliot has attempted in the Interlude of *Murder in the Cathedral* to place in the mouth of Archbishop Thomas Becket, a sermon as it might have been preached to the faithful by a man of deeds, face to face with death. Perhaps it would be hypercriticism to feel that we have here the simplicity of art rather than that of nature, as in its touching closing words:

"I have spoken to you to-day, dear children of God, of the martyrs of the past, asking you to remember especially our martyr of Canterbury, the blessed Archbishop Elphege; because it is fitting, on Christ's birth day, to remember what is that Peace which He brought; and because, dear children, I do not think I shall ever preach to you again; and because it is possible that in a short time you may have yet another martyr, and that one perhaps not the last. I would have you keep in your hearts these words that I say, and think of them at another time. In the Name of the Father, and of the Son, and of the Holy Ghost. Amen." [21]

"Epitaphs on the Church" might be the heading of another part of this collection opening with Edward Carpenter's *York Minster*, which keens at the church's wake after the long history of Christianity:

"All the preaching and the prayers and the psalm-singing of centuries have come to this;
All the rapt outpourings of the soul to God, and hidden yearnings of ages, to this?
The Church is dead. Snow covers the ground. Snug in their firelit homes, with closed shutters and surrounded by every luxury, the Wealthy the Pious and the Respectable sit—
And without, the People are dying of cold and starvation." . . .
"But hark now; from behind the screen the droning mumble of morning prayers!
It ceases, and the thin boy-voices of the scanty choir take up the chant.

Strangely from its invisible source, like some river once running strong but now losing itself in runlets in the sand,

As from out the old mediaeval world, faint and far comes sounding that refrain—

The quaint barbaric tentative uncertain-toned Gregoric refrain, soaring,

Soaring, soaring, through the great desolate nave wandering, in the ears of the one drowsy verger dying." [22]

The section which includes descriptions of the state of mind of the preacher and congregation would be illuminated by some passages from the sermons of John Donne: "I am here speaking to you, and yet I consider by the way, in the same instant, what it is likely you will say to one another, when I have done, you are not all here neither; you are here now, hearing me, and yet you are thinking that you have heard a better sermon somewhere else of this text before; you are here, and yet you think you could have heard some other doctrine of downright *Predestination* and *Reprobation* roundly delivered somewhere else with more edification to you; you are here, and you remember yourselves that now yee think of it: This had been the fittest time, now, when everybody else is at church, to have made such a private visit; and because you would bee there, you are there."

Here also one would find passages from *A Priest to the Temple* by George Herbert, "The country parson preacheth constantly, the pulpit is his joy and his throne. When he preacheth, he procures attention by all possible art, both by earnestness of speech—and by

a diligent and busy cast of his eye on his auditors, with
letting them know that he observes who marks, and
who not; and with particularizing of his speech now
to the younger sort, then to the elder, now to the
poor, and now to the rich. This is for you, and this is
for you; for particulars ever touch, and awake
more than generals. Sometimes he tells them stories,
and sayings of others, according as his text invites
him; for them also men heed, and remember better
than exhortations; which though earnest, yet often
die with the sermon, especially with country people;
which are thick, and heavy, and hard to raise to a
point of zeal, and fervency, and need a mountain of
fire to kindle them; but stories and sayings they will
well remember." [23]

Nothing will be of greater comfort to the preacher
than some knowledge of the behavior of congregations in the past as recorded for us in the records of
previous days. In the mandate from Bishop Grandisson to the Dean and Subdean after his visitation to
Exeter Cathedral on October 15, 1330, there is a picture of congregation and choir behavior which ought
to console the minister of today in meeting his very
minor problems: "We have learned from the lips of
men worthy of credit, not without grave displeasure,
that certain Vicars and other Ministers of our Cathedral Church—to the offence of God and the notable
hindrance of divine service and their own damnation
and the scandal of our Cathedral Church aforesaid—
fear not to exercise irreverently and damnably certain
disorders, laughings, gigglings, and other breaches of

discipline, during the solemn services of the church; which is shameful to relate and horrible to hear. To specify some out of many cases, those who stand at the upper stalls in the choir, and have lights within their reach at mattins, knowingly and purposely throw drippings or snuffings from the candles upon the heads or the hair of such as stand at the lower stalls, with the purpose of exciting laughter and perhaps of generating discord, or at least rancour of heart and silent hatred among the ministers (which God forfend!), at the instigation of the enemy of mankind, who (as we find by experience) knoweth and striveth to create the greatest evils not from unlawful or greater occasions only, but even from the least and most lawful. *Item*, whereas some ministers do sometimes (and, as we grieve to say, too often) commit plain faults in singing or reading incorrectly, then others who know better, (and who should rather have compassion on the ignorant and bewail the defects of their brethren), break out, in the hearing of many, into this speech of imprecation and derision in the vulgar tongue: 'Cursed be he who told the last lie!' *Item*, some whose heart is in the market-place, street, or bed, though their body be in the choir, seeking for their own part to hasten through God's work negligently and fraudulently, or to draw others as accomplices into the same fault—these (I say) will sometimes cry aloud in the English tongue to the very officiant himself, or to others, commanding and enjoining them to make haste. *Item*, sometimes, commencing the service off-hand, some show no sort of shame in beginning again

and again one service, while others begin another,
(as for instance an Anthem or Responsory or such-
like), with the accompaniment of quarrels and dis-
cords. There is yet another sin less of commission than
of omission, which hath here become a rooted custom,
and whereto in the past (if ye remember), we ourselves personally brought what we thought to be a
sufficient remedy, not only by plain admonitions but
by alluring indulgences, yet which hath now broken
out yet worse through men's negligence: namely, that
very few remain in the Choir during the Mattins of
Mary, that Blessed, Glorious, and Sweetest Mother of
Mercy, not considering that (though perchance some
may say them more distinctly outside, as some judge
of themselves, than together in the Choir, on account
of the murmurs and tumult of divers and discordant
voices) yet to God and His Blessed Mother the gift
of prayers offered by all together is incomparably
more acceptable than the same prayers said or chanted
separately in streets and corners, both as commend-
ing the unity of the Church, and also for the humble
observance of the custom, statute, and precept, and
on account of the presentation (as the Apostle saith)
of many faces, and because it may chance that each
deserveth not to be heard by himself, yet no faithful
man doubteth that he may be helped by the accordant
prayers of persons acceptable to God as there present
in common with him." [24]

Similar passages might be quoted concerning the
poor attendance at church services in medieval England as compared with shows and amusements; of

dancers who interrupted open-air sermons with their songs; of the impermanence of the results of sacred oratory; of the evils of sectarianism and preaching rivalry and sheep-stealing of competing orders of the clergy; of troubles with travelling evangelists who "tacitly deluded their audiences into the belief that they possess special authority to give a general absolution beyond anything in the power of the ordinary curate;" and of mountebank preachers who attracted large congregations by playing to the vulgar gallery. The modern preacher will rise from a perusal of Owst's "Preaching in Medieval England" feeling that his problems are not so much due to these present difficult times as he had thought.

The anthology should include even contemporary times. In its consciously and unconsciously humorous section certainly selections from H. G. Wells' bishops and clergymen, pondering sermons on what their author thinks is the newest version of God, the Invisible King; it should perhaps include the devastating conclusion to Sinclair Lewis's *Elmer Gantry*, written by a man who seems all the time to be slightly uneasy lest his readers may suppose that he is taken in by any phase of modern life, who is over-anxious to prove that he knows the best but believes the worst. Some of his strangely disturbing allusions to sermons will however find their way into such an anthology: "He had learned how to assemble Jewish texts, Greek philosophy, and Middle-Western evangelistic anecdotes into a sermon. And he had learned that poverty is blessed, but that bankers make the best deacons." The spirit of Voltaire guides the pen of Don Marquis in his frightful story entitled "Satan Goes to Church," at the conclusion of which the clergyman and the capitalist agree that "for the good of the church" they will have to let the devil remain "since he is always intruding in a business way, you know." The devil smiles. "I knew," he said, "that I wouldn't need to say anything. They always work around to the right point of view if you leave them to themselves." [25]

There is rich material in Trollope's archdeacons and curates, in Lionel Johnson's picture of the church, "Alone with Christ, desolate else, left by mankind," in Dr. Johnson's commendation of the new Methodist preachers, because they express themselves in a plain and familiar manner, "which is the only way to do good to the common people," and "for which they will be praised by men of sense." To which Boswell appends the delightful note, "Johnson himself was, in a dignified manner, a Methodist." Rich material also for the humorous section in Johnson's remark about a woman's preaching, "that it is like a dog's walking on its hind legs. It is not done well; but you are surprised to find it done at all;" in his advice as to cultivating a good style, "Read over your compositions, and whenever you meet with a passage which you think is particularly fine, strike it out;" [26] in Emerson's summation of his Divinity School address: "I told them that the preacher should be a poet smit with love of the harmonies of moral nature. A minister nowadays is plainest prose, the prose of prose. He is a warming-pan, a night-chair at sickbeds and rheumatic souls; and the fire of the minstrel's eye and the vivacity of his word is exchanged for intense, grumbling enunciation of the Cambridge sort, and for Scripture phraseology;" [27] in Thoreau's spleen against the profession, "the best preachers are an effeminate class; their bravest thoughts wear petticoats," [28] and in something from Robert Louis Stevenson's essays, from Tom Sawyer's experiences in church, George Bernard Shaw's prefaces, Newman's sermons and Samuel Butler's notebooks.

Such an Anthology of Church-going would also bring home to the minister's mind that nearly all his problems are very ancient and that his predecessors have struggled with them in their day with his own indifferent success. Dr. Owst quotes from the sermon delivered about the year 1345 in London by Archbishop Fitzralph of Armagh, in which all the perplexities of the modern minister's relation to war are exemplified: The congregation are told that they should pray that the King "may obtain a just and happy issue in his military campaigns," but the preacher adds "men pray improvidently that he may overcome his enemies, and also slay in battle. For those who pray thus, in their praying offend God, and hinder their lord the king. They offend God, in acting contrary to his command—'Thou shalt love thy neighbor as thyself' . . . They hinder the king withdrawing from him their *spiritual* petitions." Men who pray that God may "pour out the blood of their adversaries" are violating the rule of prayer "that each shall seek and pray for *all* men that which they would desire to be done to them by others," "there is no one who would desire that others would pray for them in the aforesaid fashion." But when later in the sermon the preacher comes to the objections of the pacifists of the day who think that there is no good reason for attacking France across the channel, the preacher anticipates the "making the world safe for democracy" plea, by telling his congregation that England and France are properly one kingdom the indivisible realm and dominion of the English king, which justice demands he control. The spiritual seer was able to penetrate so deeply into the truth as to be able to see that a religious man who prayed that the king might slay his enemies was hindering the king, because in so doing he was withdrawing from the king his "spiritual petitions," and yet at the close of his sermon he simply had to say a few words as an Englishman rather than as a religious man.[29]

But perhaps the last two quotations might be taken from two recent presidents of the United States. Woodrow Wilson in one of his letters writes: "I am rested, mind and body, after the morning in church. How seriously quiet Life's waters seemed when there. Over and over again I have thought of those beautiful verses of Keats:

> Upon a Sabbath-day it fell;
> Twice holy was the Sabbath bell,
> That called the folk to evening prayer;
> The city streets were clean and fair
> From wholesome drench of April rains;
> And, on the western window panes,

The chilly sunset faintly told
Of unmatured green vallies cold,
Of the green thorny bloomless hedge,
Of rivers new with spring-tide sedge,
Of primroses by shelter'd rills,
And daisies on the aguish hills.
Twice holy was the Sabbath-bell:
The silent streets were crowded well
With staid and pious companies,
Warm from their fireside orat'ries;
And moving with demurest air,
To even-song and vesper prayer.
Each arched porch, and entry low,
Was filled with patient folk and slow,
With whispers hush, and shuffling feet,
While plays the organ loud and sweet." [30]

Mrs. Reid writes: "I know of no appraisement of Woodrow Wilson that portrays his ultimate inherited quality as well as do these lines of Keats." [31]

The final entry might well be one of the famous brief after-church remarks of Calvin Coolidge to the effect that from that morning's sermon on sin, he had gathered that the minister was against it.

Such a skeleton anthology of church-going among the English-speaking peoples brings home to us a curious fact.[32] If the best literature of a people reflects the best in their national life, then in such an anthology we ought to find the deep impressions made by the habit of church-going upon the English and American peoples. As the minister reflects upon such an historic survey of English literature, it is some-

what disconcerting to find that the impression made
by church-going upon this group of men of literature
has been of three kinds: (1) Appreciation of the
friendliness or inspiration of the congregation in common prayer, in meeting together, and the impressive-
ness of the ritual observances, (2) A sense of hopeless
futility about the church as an institution of any value
to the world of the day, and (3) Humorous and
patronizing criticism, when either is mentioned at
all, of the sermon and of the preacher. It is almost impossible to discover in great English literature any
sense of the glory of preaching, any touch of the impressions made on men of imagination and literary
power by the inspired preaching of the word of God.
It is an awful thought for English-speaking preachers
that in the whole of the encyclopedic-minded Shakespeare, whose works are a mine of reference to every
interest of human life, there is not a single legitimate
reference to a sermon, to preaching or to preachers.[33]
It seems that among literary men you either have
William Watson's attitude in his verses on "The
Church To-Day":

> Outwardly splendid as of old——
> Inwardly sparkless, void and cold——
> Her force and fire all spent and gone——
> Like the dead moon, she still shines on.[34]

or simple pleasure in the company of people walking
to church, or sitting together in it, or coming away
from it. The sermon is hardly mentioned in literature

except humorously. The reason in part is that there
has been so seldom a union of real humanity and skill
in sermons. Striving to be divine the preacher ceased
to be natural and humanly interesting. Even when
there was an impression made at the time, it was not
robust enough to be remembered in tranquillity. As
one writer says: "Sermons do not often survive as
literature. The worst fault of the sermon, as literature, is that it is preaching. We make it a reproach
against writers when they preach, not merely because
preaching is out of place except in sermons, but because in itself it is disagreeable. We do not like a man
who preaches, in the pulpit or out of it; for in the
process he ceases to be human—men are not born to
preach to each other; he loses the good faith of the
artist, he tells us not what he has to say, but what he
thinks will be good for us. The convention of sermons changes, but it is never a good one; it is always
a giant's robe, awkwardly worn by a man as dwarfish
as the rest of us. When he enters the pulpit the priest
must pretend to be a prophet. However humble he be
by nature, that pretence makes him speak with alien
jaws, louder than his wont, with a solemnity that is
not his and a conviction he has not earned." [35] These
words ought to be duly weighed without resentment
by all preachers, but they do not tell the whole truth.
The fact is that the atmosphere produced by great
preaching is not communicable by literature any more
than the atmosphere of the classroom of a great
teacher. Book after book has been written by devoted

students to tell others about the greatness of some teacher of theirs, but aside from a few quaint anecdotes they have all failed to reproduce the effects which were so evidently produced in the minds of the students at the time. It is also true that preaching is a form of art designed to appeal to the simple-hearted rather than to the highly sophisticated. It is this which makes it one of the most difficult arts to practice. When one reads words like those quoted above, which resent all preaching of any kind, one is reminded of one famous Oxford don who felt he had to leave England every March "to avoid the raw greens of the English spring." It may be unnatural for a man like John Donne to get up on Sunday and tell his people that he has felt during the week "that true joy in this world shall flow into the joy of Heaven as a river flows into the sea," but it is no more unnatural than for a barren wintry countryside to let the sun inveigle it into bursting forth into a riot of green. It has also to be remembered that a truly successful sermon is a part of a whole rather than a whole in itself. The remark which a preacher should value most after a Sunday morning's work is not "What a wonderful sermon!" but "What a wonderful service!" The more sincere the sermon has been, the less does it seem to lend itself to praise or flattery. As well might a nursing infant compliment its mother on the quality of the milk, the word "applause" does not occur in brackets after the Sermon on the Mount, but you hear what they said to themselves and to each other about the teaching. It is only when there is something wrong with it, when in the old English phrase, "it sticks out like a sore thumb," that the sermon which ought to be part of life becomes separately noticeable. At its best it is an almost indistinguishable part of a personality, an integral part of a service of worship.

CHAPTER IV

THE TOOLS

HISTORY as well as literature is full of pictures which will bring home to the preacher the rich and ancient tradition to which he is an heir. The church service at which he is to officiate is not merely a contemporary and somewhat despised town or village affair, it is part of a noble tradition which, especially among the English-speaking peoples, is one with its whole history. Historic and dramatic church scenes fill the pages of history. On the twenty-third of July 1637 King Charles and Archbishop Laud decided to have a modified form of the Anglican Prayer-book used for the first time in St. Giles' Church in Edinburgh. To the Scotch people such a liturgy was a "Mass-book," the Anglican Church was a limb of Antichrist. When the reading of the liturgy started, tradition has it that Jenny Geddes arose and threw the stool on which she had been sitting at the preacher's head, at any rate there broke loose in old St. Giles' the riot which showed the righteous rage of a people whose covenant was with God rather than with man.

Those are great days to look back upon in our times. The gulf then lay between those who affirmed

and those who denied, in our time it lies between those
who affirm and those who ignore. One foreign priest
was found recently leaving the United States for his
home land, he said he was going back to a country
"where a man could have stones clodded at him for
what he believed." It is heartening to think of older
days when men had beliefs worth fighting for, worth
dying for. Perhaps in some European countries today
we see the return of such valiant hours. Perhaps in our
own land the social rather than the theoretic aspects
of religion will lead to the return of such men as John
Knox. In the year 1570 he was "lying half-dead" in
St. Andrews. But the liberty of the church was threatened, he could not cease from preaching. James Melville, an eye-witness tells us in his *Memoirs*, Knox had
to be "lifted into the pulpit, where he behoved to lean
at his first entry; but ere he had done, he was like to
ding that pulpit in blads and flee out of it." [1] The
voice of the pulpit in English history has indeed been
the voice of "saints, apostles, prophets, martyrs." To
skip over the centuries, think of those scenes in St.
Mary's in Oxford when Newman was preaching. The
nation and the age seem in them to come to some sort
of final and exquisite flower. Hear the description of
the scene from one who was present there: "To see
Newman come into St. Mary's, in his long white sur-
plice, was like nothing one had seen before. He glided
in swiftly like a spirit incarnate. When he reached
the lectern, he would drop down on his knees and remain fixed in mental prayer for a few moments, then
he rose in the same unearthly way and began the serv-

ice. His reading of the lessons from the Old and New Testaments was a most marvellous expression of soul. Many men are expressive readers, only we can see that they intend to be expressive. But they do not reach the soul; they are good actors, certainly, but they do not forget themselves, and you do not forget them. The effect of Newman's preaching on us young men was to turn our souls inside out. It was like what he says in the *Dream of Gerontius* of the soul after death, and presented before God——

> Who draws the soul from out its case
> And burns away its stains.

We could never be the same men we were before." Another member of his congregation says: "Action in the common sense there was none. His hands were literally not seen from the beginning to the end. The sermon began in a calm, musical voice, the key slightly rising as it went on; by and by the preacher warmed with his subject, till it seemed as if his very soul and body glowed with supressed emotion. The very tones of his voice seemed as if they were something more than his own. . . . The great church, the congregation all breathless with expectant attention . . . themselves perhaps standing in the half-darkness under the gallery, and then the pause before those words . . . thrilled through them, 'They say unto Him, "We are able." ' " To us as we read them in cold print it seems perhaps as if the preacher were in quest not of truth, but of the best system. They do not move us so greatly today, but historically in them a whole age came to a noble understanding of its best self.[2]

With some such sense of the great tradition which provides for him his church and his congregation, and of his relation to it and to them, the minister at last sits down to write out his sermon. It is all the way a thing is said. God must be served by adverbs. George Herbert gives a counsel of perfection to congregations when he says of preachers:

The worst speak something good: if all want sense,
    God takes a text, and preacheth patience.[3]

Many a pew has compensated for the lack of sense in the pulpit by listening to inner sermons, some of which were not preached by God. But the modern reaction to poor preaching is not patience, but absence. Still more irritating than mere lack of sense, which has its charms, is the feeling in the mind of the auditor that a good idea is struggling for expression, but is unable either to get out or get over. This state of affairs is due to a superstition on the part of a preacher that to have a good idea is to have a sermon. Much work is necessary before a good idea in your mind can be transferred to my mind. It is on this task that the minister who sits down to write out his idea is engaged. "He who speaks with understanding," says Heraclitus, "must take his foothold on what is common to all." As long as the Bible was common knowledge, the incident from which the text was taken served for such a starting point of common interest.

Such audiences may still exist in homes for aged people, but usually it is unwise to count on a modern audience ever having heard of the selected passage of Scripture before. The preacher can no longer count upon the pleasant settling down of the congregation to see what he can do with it, as he announces for his text the familiar but unpromising words "And he made a covering for the tent of rams' skins dyed red." Exodus 36:19. He may so announce a text and look around as of old, competent and challenging, about to accomplish the impossible. But nowadays all the fun is in his own mind. The congregation is not alive to the niceties of exegesis. They are only bored at the trick of getting them there for such stupidity. The sermon used to be like the Greek drama, original treatment of material familiar to all. Today the sermon which opens with a description of Corinth or a discussion of the exact theological position of the Saducees, is doomed from the start. A Cambridge Scholar is seen in an old number of *Punch,* facing from a country pulpit a congregation of farmers in smock-frocks, with the words: "But, you may quote Eusebius against me." This contingency is as unlikely as that the contemporary audience will remain awake long enough to get the chief points about Corinth or the Saducees fixed in their minds. The idea in which the sermon was born may be lofty and exalted, but a start must be made towards reaching it on common ground. Swift opened one of his sermons by reading the text and then adding "I deny that!" In his day that caught the attention of the people.

A study of the art of writing short stories as it has been developed in the last twenty-five years, is of great value to a public speaker. The problem there is very similar, how to produce in the mind of the reader the desired atmosphere for the appreciation of the incident to be recorded, without the tedious railroad journey of an introduction. Scott could say to the readers of his novels, Now I promise you a good time when you get to the story, but in all fairness, you can see the necessity for a few chapters of introductory material first. The readers of his day were so thrilled to get the story that they willingly paid the price of the historical orientation. Today you do not have to go to the barn and hitch the horse into the buggy and drive two hours in order to see a friend, you simply lift up the receiver of the telephone. The public accustomed to telephone and movies is impatient of all unnecessary preliminaries. A sermon should start when it begins. The opening sentence of an address delivered by a famous Irishman to a great audience once brought down the house, he said "Before I begin to speak, I want to say—" and the crowd laughed, but his state of mind is in essence the besetting sin of the average public speaker. Only a skilled speaker can make an effective short address, the average man has not begun what he had to say when his time is up. The first three minutes of a sermon decide whether the average man in the congregation will follow its line of thought or his own. Young people especially are so accustomed to studying with the radio on, that some of them find the obbligato of a sermon being preached in their vicinity as an enrichment of their own state of reverie. To get people to listen one must follow the demand of Pliny, the younger: "Either say something that I never read or heard before, or else hold thy peace!" [4]

It is the desire to get and to hold an audience which produces the sensational preacher, and there always have been preachers who in this respect redouble their efforts when they have forgotten their aim. Collectors of Incunabula have wondered at the number of early printed books which are works of one Roberto Caracciolo, whose name they are unable to find even in the Encyclopedia Britannica. He was one of the most sensational preachers of his day, preaching oftentimes to congregations of fifteen thousand people, and holding their attention for sermons of four hours in length. Many of the earliest printed books made just after the invention of printing were volumes of his sermons, published for the use that Sir Roger de Coverley recommended, that they might be preached by other parsons. This friend of Cosimo Medici used most picturesque methods for holding the attention of his congregations, in Holy Week in Perugia, he had himself crucified in the main square during his sermon, presumably without the nails passing through his hands; on another occasion he dressed himself up as a policeman putting his vestments over the uniform, and at an appropriate time in the sermon cried, "Who will help you against these foes?" Here he pulled off his vestments and shouted: "I am the gendarmerie!" But his very name is forgotten, so that it is almost impossible today to find anything about him without delving into the most out-of-the-way corners of antiquity. As one reads his sermons today, one is convinced that his sensational methods of delivery were necessary for him to cover up the paucity and drabness of thought and feeling.[5] Nothing is ever quite as dead as a dead sermon. But a corpse can be manipulated with strings and lights so as to collect a crowd. A bull in a china shop must be exceedingly amusing if you are not interested in the china. The great opportunity of vulgarity is the chance to desecrate some sanctity like a church or a sacred text which has been consecrated by the labor and tenderness of others. Picturesqueness, dramatic art, contemporary illustration, irony, humor, personal anecdotes, exaggerated emphasis, all have their place in preaching to ordinary people, but the aim of the sermon, the end of the effort must always be spiritual, lofty, tender, human, with more of the breath of Galilee than of Hollywood about it. It is easy to get a laugh in a place of sacred associations by feeble improprieties which could not stand the faintest breeze of out-of-door air.

Yet nature in its infinite variety has produced, every now and again in the past, sensationally dramatic preachers of great powers both emotionally and often religiously. Thomas De Witt Talmage in America and Joseph Parker in England were men of originality and with a genius for the dramatic presentation in the pulpit of religious truth. The stories of their extraordinary gifts in this direction ought to be gathered together from the fleeting memories of their congregations before it is too late. They generally did not stoop to bring objects of interest into the pulpit, like the Elizabethan playwrights they needed no scenery. One colored orator expressed himself when asked if his lecture was illustrated with stereopticon slides, "You don't need no pictures when I talk!" This was true of their preaching. Two examples of their art may be cited. Dr. Joseph Parker was minister of the City Temple in London at the height of the Science-versus-Religion controversy, when also the destructive results of the Higher Criticism were being talked and written about in England. He stands in his pulpit with the open Bible before him, and with his mind's eye greets Wellhausen, Huxley, Darwin and other scholars. The congregation can almost believe they see these critics stand together before the pulpit and the preacher's voice sounds like their voices as they each one testify that the Bible is untrustworthy in its science and its history. The preacher receives the testimony of each in its most destructive form. After all the critics have had their say, there seems very little left of the Bible. This seems to trouble the preacher, but he must be fair-minded. So, following their testimony, he closes the pulpit Bible, takes it up, turns round and throws it disrespectfully away in a negligent manner on to the seat which is ten feet or so in the rear. He then stands for what seems to the congregation a long time after this rejection of the Bible in visible perplexity, there is a good deal of sad silence, of regretful monologue. But after all the sense of the

meeting seems to be that there is no use fooling oneself. The scientists have spoken, they must be relied
on, they seem to be still standing in front of the
preacher, but he stands before a desk on which there
is no Bible. It is a sad situation. But then a new character appears in the drama. This time it is a poor
woman, a widow, who appears in great distress over
a dying baby, or an erring child. She asks the preacher
what she is to do in her terrible situation, she needs
comfort, advice, help. The preacher turns to the scientists and scholars in this crisis, they each in turn say
their say, learned chaff, well meant for grain, meaning
nothing to the poor widow. The preacher asks them
if this is all they have to give her. They admit their
inability to be of help to her in this emergency. There
is another pause. Then the preacher remembers the
rejected Bible. Slowly he turns round and walks back,
bends down and takes the Bible up, clasped in his
arms, and replaces it in the pulpit. He opens it with
expectation, he seems to caress it with affection, he
begins to read from it passages of wonderful tenderness, insight, wisdom and comfort. The light of
heaven, the good news of the gospel seem to break on
widow and preacher and congregation alike.

Or the scene is in the Brooklyn Church of Thomas
De Witt Talmage. The preacher is trying to bring
home to his congregation the fact that God loves each
one of them with a tender personal affection as if each
soul was his only child. But how can God love each
one of us so individually when we are so many? Lo!
the congregation is transferred into the home of an-

other poor widow, whose husband has just been killed
in an accident at the mill where he works. She has a
large family of children. She has no money with
which to support them. But a wealthy lady appears
before the mind's eyes of the congregation willing to
adopt one of the children. The widow must choose
which of her children she will give to this lady and
promise never to see again. It is a wonderful opportunity. It will be for the best interests of the child
and of the whole family. So the preacher shows you
the widow ranging up her children in a row to choose
which one she will give away. The preacher names
them each by name. There is Robert, her first-born,
a fine upstanding lad doing well at school. There is
Mary with the freckles on her nose, and red-headed
George, and Sammy who is lame, and Lucy with the
dimple, and so on down the family to the baby. They
are named over and over again, never forgetting, the
freckles on the nose, or the dimple on the chin, as the
widow tries to decide which of her children she can
pick out as the one she loves least, with which one
she can bear to part. The congregation lives over and
over again with the mother her attempt to decide.
Which shall it be? Till at last the poor woman covers
her face with her hands and cries out: "My God! I
can't do it!"

These examples of sensational preaching may have
been printed somewhere, they are given here not accurately, but as they are remembered after many years
by one who heard them related by one of the congregation present when they were enacted. Such dramatic

preaching has lost some of its power owing to the fact that the congregation of today has become less responsive to such appeals. The movies have preempted the ground with their far greater facilities for dramatic representation. Yet in cities where there are large crowds of ordinary folk, one cannot but believe that there is still a place for the presentation of the gospel along the lines of this ancient tradition by those specially fitted to bring home to people who are not great readers, the deepest truths of the gospel. One has to be another Beatrice Herford to be able to do it well, but when done well, its effect even today is great.

Similar were the startlingly dramatic asides with which the Scottish preachers of another generation used to interlard the reading of the Scriptures at a time when it was felt to be ritualistic to read the Lesson without comment. For the rebellion against idle repetitions went so far as to make it illegal at one time in the Scotch churches to read the Scriptures without comment. The feeling was the same as that noticeable in earlier days among the non-ritualistic churches in this country. It is not so many years ago that a minister telling of his methods of interesting his people said that in the Sacrament of the Lord's Supper he frequently varied the sequence and put the wine before the bread, "in order that we may not get into a rut about it." So in Scottish churches the minister was required to expound and apply the verses of Scripture as he went along in the reading. The writer has heard in one of these churches the preacher interject into the reading thus: "Give unto the Lord the glory due unto his name: bring an offering. A ha'penny, the sixteenth of what ye spent for tabacca last week!" And then solemnly proceed with the next scripture sentence. Dramatic remarks were sometimes made from the pulpit to special occupants of the pew. In one historic Scottish church in Ireland the Sovereign, that is to say the representative of the King used to be seated in splendor in a raised dais or pew in full view of the congregation. Pulling out his handkerchief one Sunday morning he inadvertently brought out of his pocket also a pack of cards which cascaded down his lap and over the top of the pew into the aisle, the preacher paused to look at them and remarked to the fine gentleman, "Eh, Man, yer psalmbook's ill bound!"

Ritualistic brethren and small boys have sometimes criticized the dullness and inactivity of non-ritualistic services, and have expressed themselves as feeling "that the religious value of sitting still has been grossly overestimated." But even in the days of protracted sitting still in church there were such pleasant interludes at times, dramatic scenes either in the pulpit or out of it, which should not be forgotten.

The preacher should take Whitman's advice and mingle much with ordinary people, and see if in ordinary conversation, they would be interested in the type of thing with which he was about to start his sermon. Of course it cannot be done, as Wordsworth, or at least his readers, discovered, when he tried to consistently apply his dictum that the language for poetry is the "language really used by men;" but his attempt to get rid of affectation in diction was sound and had a salutary influence on all literature. Yet "to choose incidents and situations from common life, and to relate or describe them throughout, as far as was possible in a selection of language really used by men," [6] this cannot wholly be carried out either in poetry or religion. It is for this reason that it is usually a mistake to use modern versions of the Bible in the pulpit. The King James version of the Bible was written by men who were profoundly moved by that which they were translating, and the language they used was moulded in an age most sensitive to those overtones of sound and meaning, which slip through mere single words and escape. While the preacher should begin his sermon as near the ordinary level as possible, he will find that he must rise from it as he proceeds. It is impossible to speak sensibly or accurately of art or philosophy or even baseball in the language of the ordinary man; this is even more true of religion. The attempt to throw over the entire language of religion as it has grown and matured in the experience of generations, and substitute for it the language of the ordinary man of today has a value as one man's commentary upon the words of the text of the Bible, but for common religious use more is lost than is gained by saying that "Jesus burst into tears" in order to avoid the archaic sound of the older word "wept," or by allowing the temporary (already largely discarded) use of the word "charity" for official philanthropy to force one to substitute for it the more sexually implicated word "love," or to spoil the subtle euphony of prose greater than any other ever written in English by changing "mirror," for "glass," or "guideth" for "leadeth." One is reminded of the remark made by Lefèvre on the publication of Erasmus's *Paraphrases:* "It is dangerous to try to be more elegant than the Holy Spirit." [7]

From this point of view it seems to be an unpardonable sin to change that sentence which Mr. Walter Pater once pointed out to Mrs. Humphrey Ward as an example of what he meant when he felt that orthodox religion had nothing to fear from the assault of science on the one hand and of literature on the other, that sentence which he quoted to her with the comment, "There's a mystery in it—a something supernatural." "Come unto me, all ye that labour and are heavy laden, and I will give you rest. Take my yoke upon you, and learn of me; for I am meek and lowly in heart: and ye shall find rest unto your souls. For my yoke is easy, and my burden is light." [8] It is horrible to remember that hundreds of pulpits give to their people today instead of these memorable and moving words, the advertising man's promise of the modern versions that if you "come to me," "you will find your souls refreshed." [9]

It may be said without great unfairness that the King James version is the wellspring of nearly all that is greatest in the religion of the English-speaking peoples, that the two Revised Versions were translations by philologists of words they found in the original texts,[10] and that later modern-language versions bear the same relation to the King James version that a tin cup full of water piped out of a faucet does to the last of a series of living springs from which it was taken, more practical for many uses, perhaps with fewer impurities, but emphatically tin-cup pipe water rather than spring water. The place for the modern versions is in the study, especially for the minister who has little knowledge of the original languages. The very differences between them will bring home to him the fact of the unsureness of our knowledge both of the earthly and of the heavenly Christ, due not merely to the fact that all the authors who tell us about him are interested in proving something from the data in their possession, rather than in giving the facts, but also to our ignorance of the meaning of the words they use. How much doctrine has been hung on the one Greek word ἁρπαγμόν in Philippians 2:6, and how little does anyone know as to the meaning of that rare and difficult word.

In writing the sermon, as in the initial flash of the idea, and in its delivery one has to distinguish between the genuine experience of inspiration, "a peculiar influence upon certain persons, issuing in speech or in writing of which they otherwise would be incapable," and a mere pumped-up homiletic fervor. The pleasure in having got a point and the desire to make the most of it often result in the gaseous expansion of verbosity at a high rate of emotional intensity. Even in preaching one should keep to facts or at least to truth as much as possible. A preacher is not doing so if he never has to pause and cross out a paragraph, saying to himself, "after all, that is going too far, that is not

strictly true." Piety has come into disrepute largely
because of the unreality engendered in minds which
run hysterically down one track. The higher manifestations of inspiration rise not on the ruins but on
the basis of the thought and experience of a lifetime.
Homiletical fervor, if yielded to without intellectual
common-sense leads many a preacher into strange
places. Like the orator who suddenly awoke in the
pulpit to find both his arms in the air holding up "the
good ship Temperance," which somehow had left the
sea and was sailing "all over our fair land," and was
struck dumb with a sudden sense of powerlessness as
to how to get it down into the waves again, so the
preacher who deserts truth for propaganda finds himself saying things which would make him blush if he
remembered them on Monday. This is the reason of
the necessity for writing and crossing out and writing
again. As he does so he experiences the strange magic
which there is in action of any kind. Thoughts and
developments of the ideas begin to come of themselves. There is, as A. C. Bradley says, a point up to
which the man himself was at work, and a point at
which he seems to have become the channel of another power.[11] This union of the soul with the spirit
which it worships works the miracle. The writer feels
astonished, as he reads it over—how had he ever come
upon such ideas?—and the greater the inspiration, the
greater the sense of his own littleness, and the less is
he able to ascribe its operation to himself.

There is of course a place for the platitude in a sermon. But a platitude is only distasteful when delivered

in a platitudinous manner. "All the great ideas of civilized men are common property—commonplaces as most men phrase them—it is the special turn of the thought given by men of subtlety and originality that makes their power of appeal, that makes them live." [12] Theodore Roosevelt was a master in the art of delivering platitudes in an interesting and compelling way. A vivid and colorful personality can afford to indulge in an occasional truism, and is able to make you feel that every word weighs a ton. But it is the habitual set of the mind and mouth which must be avoided, the truth which you speak must be passed through your experience and your temperament in order to make it fresh and new. Every faithful pew knows the cringing horror felt in anticipation of the expected familiar conclusion of some ponderous truism just initiated by the pulpit: " 'For the Pen,' said the Vicar: and in the sententious pause which followed I felt that I would offer any gifts of gold to avert or postpone the solemn, inevitable, and yet, as it seemed to me, perfectly appalling statement that 'the Pen is mightier than the Sword'." [13]

Mr. H. W. Fowler in his invaluable book *A Dictionary of Modern English Usage*,[14] has in several places given lists which might be enlarged into a *Dictionary of Hackneyed Phrases*, for the warning of all writers and preachers, he says: "But their true use when they come into the writer's mind is as danger-signals; he should take warning that when they suggest themselves it is because what he is writing is bad stuff, or it would not need such help; let him see to the substance of his cake instead of decorating with sugar-plums." Among his list are these: "Had few equals and no superior," "More sinned against than sinning," "Not wisely but too well," "The irony of fate," "Leave severely alone," "Which would be laughable if it were not tragic," "The psychological moment." Unless the mind of the writer as he writes is vividly alive to its depths, he will fall into the use of such hackneyed expressions and fill his writing with heavy and dull metaphorical material which would demand of the hearer an imaginative effort when there has been no such effort on the part of the speaker. The hearer will balk at this unfairness and will cease to be aware of what the speaker is saying. Such writing and speaking are uninteresting, they make an impression like that of a large basket of tumbled clothes for the wash.

Dr. Alexander White of Edinburgh and Dr. George A. Gordon of Boston were two Scotchmen who had the power of making some ordinary remark like: "It is a great thing to go through life with a level head" —and causing the hearers to feel that, in saying it, they were reviewing the whole experience of a life-time, the quintessence of the wisdom of the ages. One did it with a guileless simplicity of the eternal child, the other with the slow and ponderous magnificence of a papal bull, but for both as they uttered it, it was an incandescent point, the apex of pertinent experi-ence of endless duration. The minister has to preach certain truths which people have heard before. They only become platitudes when he does not feel them as he utters them, or when he is unable to kindle his hearers with his feeling about them. One may have heard thousands of times that fire is hot, but no one really knows it until he feels it. As the preacher writes, every idea must pass through his very being, it must be thought and felt and tasted. Masefield inaugurated poetry readings in Oxford, open to all who cared to try, and noticed how some trained elocutionists spoke their pieces without effect upon the audience, while some little shop assistant from a small town would come forward, and speak the same piece, and lo! the audience saw what he was seeing as he spoke. There is a subtle underground connection between minds, especially minds in one gathering. They sense what is going on in the mind of the speaker, whether it is mere nervous memory, egoism—or a vision. It means careful preparation if this miracle is to occur. There must be no blank spaces, no mere talking till the next idea occurs, no mere platitudes, no mere words. Every part of true style is pregnant with meaning, no sentence has simply happened in. A true original style is a succession of delighted surprises. The hearer or reader thinks he is in for the usual cliché as the sentence begins, but finds it does not turn out as he expected, it has been thought about. "be good and—" one famous sentence begins, and we all know how it will conclude, "you will be a friend of God," or "people will love you," but, as you know, Mark Twain does not end it in that way, he says: "Be good and you will be lonely." "Blessed are ye—" the hearers knew what the conclusion would be, "if ye escape persecution,"—"if life crowns you with success"—but no, "Blessed are ye, when men shall revile you, and persecute you, and shall say all manner of evil against you, falsely, for my sake." These it is true are epigrammatic sayings of great souls whose words haunt the memory of mankind, and a whole sermon cannot consist of epigrams. But take any sentence at random from a great writer or speaker and you will notice immediately the absence of dead wood, the way in which it is all impregnated with thought, and every word says something. He has loaded every rift with ore.

Preaching exists because of the conviction that there is some value in the spoken word which one misses in the reading of books. If one tries to express this idea as clearly as possible and then compares the result with Newman's exposition of the same thought, one begins to appreciate the meaning of style: "If we wish to become exact and fully furnished in any branch of knowledge which is diversified and complicated, we must consult the living man and listen to his living voice. . . . No book can convey the special spirit and delicate peculiarities of its subject with that rapidity and certainty which attend on the sympathy of mind with mind, through the eyes, the look, the accent, and the manner, in casual expressions thrown off at the moment, and the unstudied turns of familiar conversation. . . . The general principles of any study you may learn by books at home; but the detail, the colour, the tone, the air, the life which makes it live in us, you must catch all these from those in whom it lives already." [15]

The preacher is a teacher, and aims to have his congregation remember what he says. Repetition has some small place in memorizing, and it should not be despised. But the phrase repeated must be carefully chosen, lest its repetition transform it into something subtly humorous. Wellesley students of thirty years ago remember still with great delight a sermon preached by a well-known minister in which the phrase, "Woman has come to the throne," was repeated too often. One repetition or summation at the close is valid, but repetition has after all only a very little to do with remembering. People remember because what they remember has many connections with what they know or are interested in. When Calvin Coolidge was called to the telephone to be told that Harding was dead and he now was President of the United States, he did not, we may be sure, call upstairs to his wife: "Grace, don't let me forget that I am President of the United States, remind me of it in the morning!" No, he knew and remembered it forever, because it was a fact linked up in so many ways with his ambitions, day-dreams, plans, ideas, fears, philosophy, religion, politics, thoughts and desires. A congregation remembers what is linked up in its mind with the things it is thinking about and dreaming of and doing, all week long. That tree survives many droughts and storms which has many roots spread out in many directions, that thought sticks in memory which is connected with many different interests in the mind. The average sincere church-goer will say he goes to get something to live by. He means some suggestions of which he will be reminded many times in ordinary life during the week. The preacher's task is so to weld his idea into the life of the hearer that whether he buys or sells, or prospers or fails, or is well or sick, or busy or idle, every now and again some thought from the sermon of last Sunday crops up with encouragement or warning or insight or wisdom or salutary irritation.

One of the most difficult problems which meets the preacher in composing his sermon is that of weaving the message into the texture of the sermon, rather than tacking it as an addendum at the end. Æsop's fables in the form in which they have come down to us have been responsible for much of this vicious arrangement of material. It is well to remember that in all probability the morals tacked on to those fables are the work of later commentators. When the fables were first spoken they bore in themselves their own message; the application was made by the hearers.

Many modern sermons remind one of these Æsop's fables in their conventional form with the added moral. One can almost feel the point at which the preacher concluded what he had to say, and paused, and said to himself: "Now I must put in something about religion in religious phraseology." Then comes the oft-used pulpit phrase, "But most important of all is it that we—" and the congregation knows what to expect. It is extraordinary what a change of atmosphere often takes place at this point. The hearers have felt that he has been saying what he is interested in and believes; at this point he is starting to say what is expected of him. The reason for this break in the texture of the sermon is that the materials have not been mixed properly in the sermon or in the minister's life. The cake is almost ready for the oven of experience when he finds some ingredients which he had forgotten about but which ought to go in, so he dumps them in at the end and gives them an emotional stir. But they do not seem to mix right with the rest of the composition. For the congregation and the preacher alike the easiest place to end a sermon is in the skies. But the most useful place to end it, with all the inspiration that the skies can give, is at the present moment; now is the day of salvation: this day is this scripture fulfilled in your ears. But only the man whose religion is deeply interfused in his life can prevent the concluding words from seeming like something dragged into a modern non-theological sermon.

CHAPTER V

REVISION AND PREPARATION

As THE preacher writes the devil is ever at his elbow. The function of the devil is to suggest that this is good enough, this generous, well-meaning "pious palaver" will please them just as well as if he were to rouse himself to think something out. Furthermore, "What good is the sermon going to do anyway?" So the preacher is brought to face the question, "Does talking to people from an elevated structure in a building with a spire on it do them any good?" "Are people's characters or views changed by what any minister can say to them in a sermon?" If the world today were interested enough in the question to reply it would languidly answer "No!" It is fashionable to believe today that enlightened self-interest is the only motive on which one can depend for any reformation of the world. Prove to people on the basis of dollars and cents that war does not pay, and prudence will result in peace. In diplomacy the best policy produces honesty. In business profits inspire service. In law wearisome delays make justice less unjust. In philosophy efficiency is the hall mark of truth. In national, international and personal matters you can only get people to do right by bringing them to understand that it is for their own selfish interest to do so. The order is inverted, so that the familiar text reads: Seek ye first all these things, and the kingdom of God and his righteousness shall be added unto you.

Even many of the wise and good have descended to this level, and this is what M. Julien Benda calls "the treason of the Clercs." By the word "Clercs" he means those of intellectual and spiritual endowments. He draws a picture of the condition of Europe in the twelfth century, when there were two distinct groups of people, determined to seize a portion of the earth. Each group was beginning to hold that "We must defend the essential part of ourselves as a class or tribe or nation." The first group was beginning to believe that one must pin one's faith for real progress to enlightened self-interest, that it was frivolous to expect anything from a moral improvement of the race. On the other hand there were men of learning, artists and philosophers, preaching the cult of the human or at least of the Christian, laboring to thwart the work of the other group, using a universal language among themselves. "Today," he says, "the game is over. Humanity is nationalized. The layman has won. But his triumph has gone beyond anything he could have expected. The 'clerc' is not only conquered, he is assimilated." This author is in some doubt whether the universal, spiritual, human point of view can ever be regained, "Peace is not the absence of war, but a virtue born from strength of soul," says Spinoza, and M. Benda adds, "Peace will not be the abstaining from

an act but the coming of a state of mind. In this sense
the most insignificant writer can serve peace where
the most powerful tribunals can do nothing." [1] The
preoccupation with things which cannot be shared as
being the essentials for happiness is the state of mind
with which the "clerc" had no sympathy. But this
religion of disinterestedness may have been just a
lucky accident in man's history, a pearl which has now
been dropped again into the ocean, with only an in-
finitesimal chance that it may ever be recovered. This
is plain speaking for all preachers who are inclined to
gain the ear of the layman by placing their "practical"
desires under the patronage of the highest spiritual
authorities.

But if the cobbler sticks to his last, if the pulpit
keeps to its point that the kingdom of Heaven and the
righteousness of God must be sought first, the question still remains: Does talking to people from an elevated structure do them any good, does it change
them at all? A fair answer to this question would be
a study of what Hitler has done to the German people
in the last few months by talking to them. The question is not as to the value of what he has done or said,
the question is as to the fact of the revolution in a
whole people's ways of thinking and acting which
has been the result of what he has said to them. Anyone who has read his own account of his early struggles to get people to listen to him, of his philosophy
of public speaking which he carried out into tremendous popular success, will not entirely give up hope
that even with a people less regimented than the

German nation, it is possible to change people by public speech. Hitler says that "all great world-shaking events were brought about not by the written but by the spoken word." "The average man is far more ready to take in a picturesque oral presentation than he is to read a lengthy treatise. The picture brings an explanation in much shorter time, I might almost say, in one flash, which he would receive only by tedious reading of the printed page." He speaks of the impossibility of reaching the heart of the masses by the written word alone. He chooses his times and places with care: "The same speech, the same speaker, the same subject work altogether differently at ten o'clock in the morning, at three o'clock in the afternoon, or in the evening . . . for I do not measure the success of a speech delivered by a statesman to his people by the effect it has upon a university professor, but by the influence which it exerts upon the people. This alone is the test of the genius of the orator." "The will, the longing, but also the power of thousands communicates itself to every member of the audience. The man who came to such a gathering doubting and wavering, leaves it firmly convinced: he has become a member of a brotherhood." Much that is cynical and meretricious mingles itself with Hitler's account of his success as a speaker, his audiences were much more desperate and more docile than any which face the average American speaker, but he at least has proved that the power of a speaker in changing the lives of his audience has not entirely faded from the earth. It cannot be believed that what one man can do with such mingled motives as his, cannot also be done even more powerfully by one of higher ideals and purer aims. Whatever the future judgment of history may be upon his life as a whole, no one can gainsay that he did in a brief period at the beginning of his career transform the temper of a whole nation by his words.[2]

The preacher can well afford to throw his ink bottle at the devil, as the stain upon the wall in the Wartburg once testified Luther was forced to do, informing that apostle of the second best, that nothing is too good for any audience. The less sophisticated the audience, the more difficult it is to speak to them with profit. One can usefully give the confused process of one's thinking to the learned, but one must win through to a certain final clarity when speaking to ordinary folk. New mechanism is not widely marketable till it is fool-proof, as long as a lengthy and intricate book of instructions as to minute adjustments which must be made in certain cases has to go with the new invention, the contraption is not really available for ordinary use. Only when people without any knowledge of the immense problems which had to be overcome in their construction could operate the automobile, the radio, the electric refrigerator, the telephone, were these inventions fit to be introduced into the regular routine of existence. As long as the preacher's material is complicated and intricate, couched in abstract terms or in philosophical or scientific slang, and tagged with various labels of minute instructions, doubts, and modifications in special cases, it is not ready for delivery, he has some more work to do upon it. When Mr. Whitehead says: "The prehension into God of each creature is directed with the subjective aim, and clothed with the subjective form, wholly derivative from his all-inclusive primordial valuation," his thought is not yet in a form suited to serve as a motto on a Christmas card, but when he says, a few pages later of God: "He does not create the world, he saves it: or, more accurately, he is the poet of the world, with tender patience leading it by his vision of truth, beauty, and goodness," [3] his thought is in a form which almost any preacher could bring home to the least sophisticated congregation.

Some preachers are apt to excuse their own unintelligibility by accusing more popular preachers of merely telling their congregations Sunday School stories, but this is not a fair statement. It may be questionable whether every truth can be put in a form intelligible to any ordinary group of people. One great mathematician was recently dared to give a popular explanation of Einstein's theories to such a group. Dr. E. T. Bell was moderately successful when he said: "The essence of Einstein's generalization is its final disentanglement of that part of any physical event which is contributed by the observer from that part which is inherent in the nature of things and independent of all observers." [4] And Dr. W. Heisenberg added a word further when he said: "Our ordinary descriptions of nature, and the idea of exact laws, rest on the assumption that it is possible to observe things without appreciably influencing them." Such valiant attempts to make the abstruse intelligible to the non-expert ought to hearten the preacher when he tries with much more tractable material to make himself understood to all of his congregation, and yet bring them the very best thought of which he is capable. Even a children's sermon which interests the youngest in the Primary Department can show to a scholarly listener that the preacher knows his Whitehead, his Freud and his Dewey, but its value to this same scholar is in the fact that the child in him is touched and enlightened by the simple talk. But people who are roused emotionally and mentally are much more able to follow the preacher into the higher reaches of his thought and emotion than is the average man on the street. Happy is that preacher who addresses an audience already moved and impressed by the dignity and beauty of the services which precede the sermon. Some kind of ritual seems necessary in all services of worship, whether it be of the "I'm a regular guy" type, "Well, fellows! Here we are again! What do you say to Hymn 198?" or the solemn stereotyped Protestant form "Let us join in reading Responsive Reading number 68," or the Catholic approach to God with "Lift up your hearts," "We lift them up unto the Lord." All are equally ritual, because it is impossible to vary them every time they are used, the only difference is that the first two brothers think they are not ritualistic because what they say every Sunday is not beautiful.

The form of the church is important but even the most unpromising environment can be overcome by the spirit of the service. It is, however, a help to all if the minister does not have to face the congregation as he prays, as though he were addressing them, if the choir likewise seems from its position to be singing to the glory of God rather than for the delectation of the people, if all who lead the worship are in attitudes suggesting that they, as well as the congregation, are engaged in their own devotions. It is excellent if the main line of vision for the congregation does not lead up to organ pipes, an electric fan, or even a pulpit, during the devotional service, but if in some symbolic way their attention is directed towards prayer rather than comfort, mechanism or criticism. People fall into the line of attention that seems expected of them by the arrangements of the building where they meet. If the pulpit is central, they settle down to see what is wrong with the sermon. If the choir or organ is the only thing they can look at, their minds are blocked by that interest. There is a great deal to be said for building a church as a place of prayer, where the attention is centered on something simple, symbolic, something which draws out of the worshipper a sense of his attitude towards the unseen. The art of common worship is the art of getting the minds and emotions of the congregation to operate, cajoling the people to do more than half the work. Everything about the opening services should suggest a whole congregation united in prayer, rather than a man or group of people speaking or singing to them. Every minister should attend with reverence and devotion many other kinds of services than his own. The Protestant minister can learn most from the immense wisdom of the Ro-

man church in fostering the spirit of devotion in the
humblest of its people, the Catholic priest can learn
most from the preaching and prayers in the Protestant churches.

No one can give much help to the minister in the
preparation of his pastoral prayer, except to suggest
that *The Dictionary of Hackneyed Phrases* be kept in
mind. Many pulpit prayer phrases mean nothing any
more, they have about them a faint odor of disin-
fectant, the word "Bless" has probably served long
enough to cover lack of thought and could be buried
in consecrated ground, the cuckoo-clock description
of parochial activity "Bless our parish visitor as she
goes in and out among us," the intensely pious par-
ticularity of "each and every one," and many other
such phrases may have tombstones there all their own,
they have been long overworked and need a long rest.
The best way to prepare for the pastoral prayer is to
read over again some of the great devotional passages
of literature in Psalms and Isaiah, or the magnificent
diction of Milton, the rhetoric of Martineau, one of
Fosdick's sermons or the *Speculum Animae* of Inge,
and then to rest the mind on the Sunday paper.

So the minister has finished writing his sermon, and
has thought of his devotional services, and lunch is
ready and there are afternoon calls to be made and a
meeting of one of the Church Eating Clubs in the
evening. He lays his manuscript down, feeling that it
is rather good and goes downstairs. It is next day or
the day after before he is able to read over his sermon
again, all the time it has been in the back of his mind

as a piece of work well done. He takes it up again. What a disappointment it is in many places, every preacher knows. "How seldom does a cup of coffee equal the idea of a cup of coffee." In the heat of composition he had not noticed that these thoughts do not jibe, these paragraphs are contradictory, no one could understand what he meant here, and there are unpardonable crudities. He knows what one great writer meant when, reading over his book which he had written in such heat, he compared the inadequacy of what he found there with the vividness and freshness of the vision in the light of which it was conceived:

"Alas! what are you now, my thoughts which I have written and painted here! It seems but a moment ago since you were so gayly colored, young and malicious, full of pricking thorns and secret spices, making me sneeze and laugh—and now?

"All your novelty has faded and some of you are on the way, I fear it, to become Truths, you look already so everlasting, so pathetically sincere, so tedious. And was it not always so?

"What are the matters which we write and paint, we mandarins with Chinese brush, we who strive to make eternal the things which can be written down, what is it in the end which is capable of being painted?

"Alas! only that which is on the point of fading and is losing its fragrance. Alas! only exhausted and departing storms, and yellowing sentiments which have come too late. Alas, only birds when their flight is over, when, lost and wearied, they are easily caught in the hand—in our hand.

"We strive to make eternal what cannot live or fly much longer, only that which is tired and overdone.

"Oh, my thoughts which I have written and painted, all my colors are for your afternoon. It is true I have many tender colors, and fifty yellows and browns and greens and reds!—but from them all nobody will guess how ye looked in your morning, ye sudden sparks and miracles of my Solitude—my old beloved—wicked thoughts!" [5]

It all seems so trite now. He wonders if he really had anything to say. But "despair is the master of impossibilities" and he goes to work revising, correcting, changing. Disappointed, and yet experiencing in some genuine degree what Robert Bridges found was true of nearly all real revision of one's own best work: "Heine's file was as full of genius as his soul, so that like Beethoven, the more he retouched his work, the nearer it approached the perfect ease of spontaneity." [6]

Much time will be spent in transposing the abstract into the concrete. Art hates the abstract and the known analogy, it loves the complex discovery of a new path through genuinely ordinary circumstances, the end of the sermon is not a demonstration, a Q.E.D.; it is the tasting of a spiritual atmosphere. It is difficult for the young preacher to slough off the abstract term, scientific slang, philosophic shorthand and academic jargon. He has been hearing and talking, for instance, of "Values," and "the world of Values" and cannot understand that these ideas must be translated into concrete forms if they are to be apprehended by the average member of his congregation. It is much easier to use them as vague algebraic symbols than it is to think up a way of explaining to himself and his congregation what he is talking about. Mr. Lin Yutang in his book *My Country and My People* gives illustrations of the hatred felt by the Chinese for abstract terms, of their picturesque way of imagining in the concrete. These are food for the meditations of the public speaker. Such words as "factors," "processes," "individualization," "departmentalization" are not found in Chinese, and instead of saying "one function of art is to quicken one's perception of nature," they say:

> First we look at the hills in the painting,
> Then we look at the painting in the hills.

Art also hates sentimentality, as a smile hates a smirk, as tears hate glycerine, so it is well to go through the sermon and delete almost all references to "my heart," in fact most references to oneself, as nearly everybody regards himself sentimentally. The minister should read his sermon aloud, as many a sentence that looks well on paper is too involved to be effective when one is speaking in an ordinary voice to others, for this reason there should be a lock on the inside of the study door, and the minister's wife may give to visitors what explanations she likes for the strange noises emanating from the sanctum upstairs. It may be necessary for her to do as Mrs. Gamp did and invent a mythical Mrs. 'Arris to whom the minister is giving a piece of his mind. This habit of reading aloud re-

sults in sermons not essays, the speaking voice not the
written style. There are two forms of intellectual exercise which are invaluable for the public speaker.
One is reading aloud, not only his own prospective
speeches but the work of others who have succeeded
in holding the attention of audiences. There is a subtle
difference between a sentence intended to be visually
read and the same truth expressed in words which are
designed to be given orally. "A phrase can only live
when it corresponds to all the necessities of respiration. I know it to be good when it can be read aloud.
Badly written sentences do not stand this test; they
weigh on your chest, hinder the beating of your heart,
and thus find themselves outside the conditions of
life." Faguet says that this is "one of the most pro-
found remarks that has ever been made concerning
the organism of style." [7] In reading one's own work
aloud before delivery, one should note whether one's
own respiration remains equal to the strain of proclaiming these weighty sentences to a congregation,
whether pauses might not be introduced, material re-
arranged, for the purpose of effective speech. Many
a good story has been spoiled by the poor telling. John
Bright said of Manning after listening to him preach
in Rome: "That man is a very good speaker if you
don't listen to what he says," but of more preachers
it might be remarked: "What he is trying to say is
good, if he only could say it."

The other mental exercise of most value to a public
speaker is translating from a foreign language. In
order to translate one has to catch the idea in a sen-

tence, then forget the words of the foreign language and translate the idea into one's own tongue. "A Translator that would write with the force and spirit of an Original, must never dwell on the words of an author," said Dryden. Now this intellectual operation is very similar to that of an extempore speaker, who should not remember words, but ideas, who, struck with a sudden splendid enlargement of his subject, can leave his manuscript and launch forth in pursuit of it before his audience. All great oratory has a spice of this adventure in it. But the translation must be serious work, written work, expressed in idiomatic English. The diligent drudgery of translating another's thoughts into English will stand the preacher in good stead when the occasion is set and souls are attuned to great issues and that happens to him which he had sought in vain in the hours of his study, the flash of inspiration, the leap of association takes place which "like the angel in the Gospel, stirs to momentary potency the waters of the pool." Every preacher is a new edition of the universe. He is translating ideas which are universal into the idiom of his own experience and his own day.

On reading over his sermon he will notice cases of special pleading, where he has not been fair to the other side. The minister should be a searcher after truth rather than a lawyer who labors to make the best of a case to which he is professionally committed. He must strive to be fair to people of whom he disapproves. The great difficulty, unsurmounted by the author of *The Pilgrim's Progress*, is to make the good life appear more attractive, even with heaven added to it, than the life in Vanity Fair. Bunyan was forced to borrow some attractions from the Fair in order to make the Celestial City seem tolerable, as for instance that "you shall be clothed with glory and majesty, and put into an equipage fit to ride out with the King of Glory," "yea, and when he shall pass sentence upon all the workers of iniquity, let them be angels or men, you also shall have a voice in that judgment, because they were his and your enemies." [8] This is the nemesis which overtakes those who are unfair in their attempt to make a case out for God. What sentimental writer of fiction would have dared to put into the mouth of the Savior on the cross the words, "My God, my God, why hast thou forsaken me?" or that fair defence of persecutors, "they know not what they do"?

He will strive to insert even into his highest flights of mystic insight some indication of what he means in ordinary language. "The cup of cold water," "I was hungry and ye fed me," "they shall beat their swords into ploughshares," "charity suffereth long and is kind," "are not two sparrows sold for a farthing? and one of them shall not fall on the ground without your Father," here ordinary words and ideas splice the golden bough of highest spiritual truth into the staff of common life.

"A young author is tempted to leave anything he has written through fear of not having enough to say if he goes cutting out too freely. But it is easier to be long than short. I have always found," says Samuel Butler, "compressing, cutting out, and tersifying a passage suggests more than anything else does. Things pruned off in this way are like the heads of the hydra, two grow for every one that is lopped off." [9]

Never more clearly than when he is correcting his sermon does the preacher realize that his task is to be both prophet and artist. The artistry of the greatest prophets is largely unconscious, it is one aspect of their flaming sincerity and earnestness. They are truly surprised and annoyed when people admire the way they say things. Ruskin in such a mood is reported to have explained his position in words like these: "I spend my time in telling the people of England that they are going straight to hell, and they respond by telling me how beautifully I write." Yet he who would speak to the needs of today must unite in himself both the prophet's fire and the ability of the artist, the longing to be counted worthy to perish for the saving of the world, the certainty of spiritual experience, the courage of real conviction, the fearlessness of truth, and yet all these may only reach and be appreciated by those already convinced unless there is added to these prophetic qualities something of the mood of the artist, which has been well described by M. Mauron: "This amused acceptance of the world and its oddities, this contemplation, at once malicious and sympathetic, which seems balanced quiveringly on the edge of laughter, pity, tenderness and gratitude." [10] When the artist predominates you have an essay. When the prophetic mood is allowed to have full sway the result is apt to be what was called during the war a "straf" sermon, a scolding. When the writer was acting as interpreter for Albert Schweitzer in Oxford, he told him of his experiences in Africa in listening to the sermons of some of the missionaries preaching to the natives. They were obsessed, he said, by the evils of native life as they saw them, and preached constantly against alcohol and polygamy, until Dr. and Mrs. Schweitzer came to anticipate the subject and the conclusion of every sermon. One day the preacher announced that, on the following Sunday, he would preach upon the Creation of the World. "Mrs. Schweitzer looked up at me," he said, "and remarked in a relieved manner, 'We shall have a holiday for one Sunday from Alcohol and Polygamy.' I looked down at her and said, 'My dear, you know little of the mysteries of exegesis.'" On the next Sunday, the preacher listed the things which God created on the successive five days of the first week, and then paused to ask his congregation this question: "I have now recounted all the things which God created, and I ask you 'Was Alcohol among the number?'" He then proceeded to the creation of Adam and Eve, and paused again to call their attention to the fact that there was only one Eve. So he managed to get his two "straf" subjects into the first sentences of his introduction.

The perfect union of the artist with the priest and prophet can be illustrated from another incident he related. It is the custom in that part of Africa to give a child a taboo just as soon as he is born. The more difficult the taboo the less likely it is that evil spirits will bother it, as, if the forbidden action is a severe deprivation and limitation of life, the evil spirits will let the child alone feeling that its life will not be much good to it anyway. It was the custom of the missionaries to preach also against this custom of taboo. They told the natives that there was absolutely nothing in it. But the natives found that owing to the fatal terror which ensued on the breaking of a taboo, there was something in it, and so came to the conclusion that these missionaries were in league with the evil spirits. Dr. Schweitzer told of seeing a young man, who had inadvertently broken his taboo, die of fright, in spite of all he could do to save him.

One day after long labor a child was born in Dr. Schweitzer's hospital. The labor had been so prolonged and terrible that it was evident to the mother that the evil spirits were particularly set upon the destruction of her child. So in this extremity, she did something which few mothers dare to do, she allowed another to give the child his taboo. She said: "Doctor, you give the child his name and his taboo." Now, instead of bending down to explain to the distracted mother that there was absolutely nothing in the taboo idea, Dr. Schweitzer said: "The child's name is Albert Doctor, and his taboo is that he shall never touch alcohol." "Thus," he said, "I killed two birds with one stone, kept her confidence and saved the boy from his greatest temptation."

There you have in one man the poet, the scholar, the prophet, the artist, the pastor, and the priest, in action in an emergency. For a long time Dr. Schweitzer was looked upon as too unorthodox to be permitted to preach, he was limited to his medical work by the authorities of the society. But at last he was allowed to preach. The writer asked him what, with his critical outlook on theology, he found himself able to preach to these simple folk. "Oh," he said, "these people are born scared, live scared, and die scared, of evil spirits. I limited myself to preaching to them that in spite of all appearances to the contrary, behind all the seeming mystery and cruelty of life, there was not terror but love, the Father of Jesus Christ."

So as an artist who respects his medium and his craft, as a prophet with a burning message in his being, the preacher finishes the correction of the manuscript of his sermon, and lays it aside, let us say, optimistically, on Friday noon. He reads it over again aloud on Saturday morning and modifies a few mixed metaphors, changes the order of some of the paragraphs, and retouches the conclusion.

The minister's Saturday night might well be spent in reading some of the eloquent expressions of religious exaltation, such as Francis Thompson's *The Hound of Heaven*, Louise Collier Wilcox's *A Manual of Spiritual Fortification*, or *The Oxford Book of Mystical English Verse*, Faber's or Whittier's *Hymns*, Milton's prose, or favorite passages from the eloquence of Newman or Phillips Brooks, or such anthologies of the yearning, tenderness, courage, faith, overwhelming mystery of prayer as are to be found for instance in that great chapter on the personal prayers of great men in Heiler's book upon *Prayer*.[11]

The atmosphere of the service on the morrow is

largely determined by the atmosphere of the minister's mind, and that somehow is subconsciously connected with the thoughts of the night before. The nadir of all preaching was reached at a time when the most popular homiletic work in the preacher's library was that volume popularly known by the droll title of *Dormi Secure*. It was fourteenth-century handbook of outline sermons for parish preachers, "who thereby might sleep out their Saturday nights in peace, in sure and certain knowledge that a message needing no prolonged preparation lay ready for them on the morrow." [12] So popular was it that the *Dictionary of National Biography* tells us that it went through more than thirty editions, at least fourteen of which may still be consulted in the British Museum today.[13]

There is a very distinct difference in the atmosphere of classrooms taught by various teachers and in the churches preached to by various preachers. Nervous emotional strain is produced by preachers who are consciously trying to pump up the temperature to the religious boiling point. The constricted tense muscles of the poor player who is vainly trying to hit a golf ball, as compared with the relaxed easy swing of the accomplished player; in this contrast one has a picture of a secret valid in the sphere of religion, and especially in the sphere of religious eloquence. In the first case we have an incompetent person trying to get up power enough to hit the ball, in the second case we have a trained athlete who takes the ball in the natural rhythmic swing of his own life. Saturday's period spent in the company of the great athletes of the spiritual world tones up the inner life of the preacher, till its swing can carry through in power. The liberal preacher cannot depend upon magic to produce the required atmosphere automatically for him. Even the sonorous repetition of the blessed word "Mesopotamia" has little effect on the congregation to which he preaches. Beauty of ritual and architecture are a help, but the message which reaches the soul of the congregation must have passed through the mind and emotion and body of the preacher. It must not merely be an occasional piece, but part of the texture of his being. As the preacher proceeds with the service the response of the congregation is like that portrayed in Kipling's *Brushwood Boy*, "Here is a man who has been where I have been," "So you have felt that way too," "You have been in my world," "It all joins on, you know—it's the same country—and it was easy enough to see where you had been."

A sermon which is a rhetorical flourish tacked on to a drab dwelling can never induce such experiences in a congregation, it only happens when the people glimpse in the sermon for a moment the glow and movement, the triumph and defeat, the comedy and tragedy of the life being lived within.

The weakness of modern art is its thinness, one feels that the author or preacher is telling you all he knows, that he is running the risk of exhausting his stock in trade. The humor of the *New Yorker* sometimes seems to be the result of a concentrated effort of an expert wise-cracker straining his abilities to the utmost, while the humor of older cultures, like the stray remarks of Dr. Johnson, appears rather as incidental sparks struck out on an anvil by one engaged in other matters. Scratch one of the older addresses or sermons and you often find a deep vein of unexpressed wisdom and experience, scratch so many modern utterances and you find an article from a popular "Digest" of a longer article from a popular magazine.

Talking about anything, telling all you know about anything which means a great deal to you seems to spoil it, seems to vulgarize it. The more human attitude is that of the lines:

> Ah, free, aff-hand yer story tell,
> When wi' yer busom crony,
> But still keep somethin' to yersel
> Ye scarcely tell to ony.

But it is the business of ministers to be talking continually about the deepest things of life. Their only hope is to cherish an inner life which is literally *hid* with Christ in God. One often wonders what it is which makes one man talking of things seem like a chatterer, while the words of another man talking of the same things seem not to be words, but windows opening on a new world: the reason for this phenomenon is that the one man is talking what he has just heard or read or what has just occurred to him, there is no background for resonance, while the other man is talking out of an inner life richly furnished with experience and thought and meditation. It is the unexpressed portion of the life which gives tone and substance to the utterances. The minister who preaches the last book or the last magazine article he has read does not need his Saturday night; after all his sermon is finished. But the minister who has a personal religious life altogether apart from professional uses finds on that evening an opportunity to worship in that inner temple of the mind of which he cannot talk. All growth is in secret. All buds are covered in a mysterious case. Touch the mystery of the setting crystal and it grows no more, remove the covering from the bud and it dies. The best of religion cannot be expressed in words, one knows it only for oneself. Goethe knew more about the workings of the mind of man in this twilight region than any modern, he says: "There are many things about which we human beings cannot make ourselves entirely understood, and so I have often to say to myself, about this matter and that I can only talk with God. . . . Let me whisper this in your ear: I have this wonderful experience that in my old age, thoughts come to me, which if I were to follow out and carry into practice, would make it worth while for me to live my whole life over again. . . . We all wander in the midst of mysteries; we grope around amid mysteries and wonders: the truth, that is the divine is never known by us directly, we see it only in reflexion, in example, in symbol, in separate and related appearances." It is this mysterious life which cannot be expressed which alone saves a minister from appearing as one who has talked himself out, from that self-contempt which a man feels who has talked about that which expression only profanes.

Anyone who has made many pilgrimages to the Adams monument at Rocky Creek Cemetery in Washington knows what Goethe meant. One wants to go alone. One does not want to say anything or to have anything said. The inexorable fact is that all that has been said about art and expression and revision are worse than useless, unless one has this other endowment about which nothing can be said. Without it the most gifted preacher is of less value than a phonograph record, for nature has never been interested in making perfect machines. Without it the audience has the same experience as when it hears over the radio the commercially cultured tones of the announcer turn from tooth-paste to read the Christmas story from the Gospels. The spark of which we speak when we talk of preachers is a spark from a fire which smoulders deep in his life. At the supreme moment of the passion we read that the sun hid his face. All real religion springs from experiences which no sun of investigation, no prattle of words can enlighten. A personal religion which has no thought of the pulpit, and never can be expressed fully therein is the making of a minister. One hesitates to describe it by any of the words used by the mystics, for so many of whom it was occult and mysterious in a sense opposed to all thought and imagination and knowledge. For us it is rather cognate with the moment of discovery in research, to the unexpected act of creation of the artist. In mathematics when one finds to one's astonishment that the well-known principle is just a special case of a far more wide-spreading law, when some analogy seems to connect suddenly distant phenomena in botany and zoology, when in an inspired moment one seems to leap into the picture and live in the world the painter imagined there, when the general aspect of reality of which the music is an expression opens up with a thousand different visions of unsuspected beauty, when one strikes reality in art at a point in the stream far above that where words begin, then one has some conception of the unexpressible religious life which is the experience of which all preaching is an echo. The most curious fact about this deep religious experience is that although it leaps over words, cannot be expressed in them, it can be expressed in deeds and in life. Its presence in a life can be felt by all. Words dangerously distort. It expresses itself only in the open secret of a life, which seems to be lived to the tune of some unheard melody.

At last the minister is in the pulpit. His position is an incredible one. He is actually expected to address God on his own behalf and that of the congregation. How shall he do so? Should he speak as a modern child would speak to a father, or as a child of one hundred years ago would speak to a father, or as a subject craving a favor would speak to an Eastern potentate, or as a man of today would ask help of a physician, or as a college president would beg for endowment from a millionaire, or as a student would seek help from a scholar, or as a drowning man would cry for aid from a passer-by? Must there be something antique and courtly about an approach to God as in a Buckingham Palace presentation, or can one follow the more democratic manners of the White House? Or should he "demonstrate" rather than pray, turn on power by obeying certain mental and spiritual laws, rather than ask for it as a favor? Or should he meditate simply, allow selected spiritual truths to sink in as they are thought over slowly by him and his congregation? Should he think of God as a person or as a principle? Should he for the sake of form open his prayer with, "O Lord, we know that—" and then deliver a short homily on some suitable theme, or with the words, "O Lord, help us to—" and then change the key to one of exhortation? If there are two hundred persons visible in the church, is he supposed to be talking to a two hundred and first person present but unseen, or is he simply adjusting himself as one minister did who arrived prepared to make a speech, and when he found he was down on the program only to lead in prayer, said in reply to apologies for the misunderstanding: "Oh, it's all right, I can throw the remarks I was going to make into the form of a prayer"?

Most inconsistently perhaps we should have to answer nearly all of these questions in the affirmative, and cover our confusion by stating loftily that similar divergence of method always exists when one treats a mystery pragmatically. In prayer we touch a power which is incomprehensible to any except one who does not believe in it. Under such conditions the best we can do is to make use of any means which prove to be practical in utilizing it. Just as the early stages of man's knowledge of electricity are a curious clutter

of magnets, and ebony wands rubbed by chamois
cloths, and lightning kites, and boxes for giving people shocks, and cats being stroked, and frictional
sparking machines, so in the early knowledge of any
mysterious force, many seemingly unrelated methods
exist side by side. So heterosuggestion, autosuggestion,
wishful thinking, imagination, exhortation, meditation, ritual, petition, praise, confession, silence, faith,
conversation, even complaint, all seem to have their
place as ways of coming into touch with this mysterious power. The question "Is there a God?" does
not come into the sphere of these lectures, and can
probably never be answered except by the disappear-
ance of the question. The existence of human society
is a much surer fact of experience than the existence
of the whole physical universe, "all of which is derivative and inferential, since it assumes the existence of
human instruments like language, mathematics, meas-
urements." [14] In experiencing something which one
cannot fully understand, one must be willing before
trying clearly to link it to one's outside universe, to
experiment with many suggested methods. It is only
when it is asserted that prayer is only one of these
methods, that one who has experienced religion dis-
sents. There is wishful thinking in prayer, but the attempt to limit prayer to that experience is simply
laughable to one who knows that much of his own
experience in prayer might be far better symbolized
by knocking one's head against an impenetrable stone
wall. There is autosuggestion in prayer but much of
the experience is more like the solving of a difficult

problem in mathematics. There is the talk of a child to a wise father in prayer, but as, for instance Rilke has pictured it, it is more like the talk of a worldly-wise father to a child.[15] Prayer is indeed talking to God about anything which you think might interest him. Part of the time, it is true, you are talking to a principle, and the reaction is automatic, in accordance with the laws of mind; but you never can tell when you go past that stage and even more mysterious results begin to stir your being. This is especially true when you can induce a whole congregation to enter into the mood with you, and when these things happen, you are on much surer ground than if you had demonstrated rationally the existence of a certain kind of a God. For after all it is about the things you think he would be interested in that you are talking, and your idea of what they would be is the quintessence of the kind of life you are living. So there are no rules for public prayer. It happens when the primitive self bursts out into an expression of its deepest loyalties and needs.

CHAPTER VI

PREACHING, DELIVERY AND RESULTS

THE great weakness of Protestantism is that the success of its services depend so entirely upon the personality of the minister. It is the perfect form of religion when a man with a touch of religious genius is conducting the service. It is much more barren and dead than the Catholic service when conducted by one without the divine fire. With the exception of the Sacrament of the Lord's Supper, Evangelical Protestantism has thrown away nearly all methods of expressing and communicating experience which cannot be expressed in words. When Luther said of the doctrine of transubstantiation, "bread remains bread—wine remains wine," he started an operation which Evangelical Protestantism has carried to its logical conclusion. He did away with the idea that certain religious truths and experiences which are far too deep and subtle for the ordinary priest to partake of or understand, can nevertheless be preserved and transmitted by that ordinary priest in sensuous and mystical symbols and ritual acts. Catholicism holds that pearls of great price can be given away by one who has himself no understanding of their beauty or value, Protestantism, on the other hand, is inclined to doubt whether pearls have any greater value or beauty than is appreciated and understood by him who is appointed to distribute them to the people. Protestantism has perhaps more right on its side than Catholicism, although as a result of this dependence upon reason and the word, there is probably less real prayer and devotion in the average Protestant church than in the average Catholic church. Yet to balance this loss, it should be said that when the method does work, when a man of real religious genius is conducting the service, the Protestant results are so much more splendid than the Catholic. It is not because there are too few religious geniuses that public prayer is such a farce in many Protestant churches, it is because the average man does not cultivate and deepen the gift of receptive and cooperative prayer that is in him. Two pictures might visit his mind as he prays, one that of the great invisible comrade in a terrific struggle, sympathetic, courageous, wise, and yet in need of the help and cooperation of men if ultimate victory is to be assured; the other that of a great power, ready and willing to pour its healing, purifying and renewing stream through the channel of our lives, if we can but bring ourselves in prayer to turn those oblique and wayward passages in the direction of his will.

Just as a Protestant often sits in trains and other public places and wonders what is going on inside the head of the priest who is so diligently reading his breviary beside him; is it a purely mechanical vibration of the optic muscles across the lines, or must the throat muscles also and perhaps the lips form chimerical images of the words, before the reading of the office is ecclesiastically valid, is the brain of the priest entirely dormant, or do some of the ideas connected with the too familiar words still filter into the mind? Would he know what he had been reading after the book had been closed? Is the total effect of the reading merely the satisfaction on the fulfilment of a duty done, as when Dr. Johnson felt that he had touched as he had promised himself each of the lampposts in a street? In a similar way many a member of a Protestant congregation sits in his pew and wonders what is going on in the mind of the minister who is leading in public prayer. Sometimes it is clear that he is merely meandering, each sentence being suggested by something in the previous one, as when "Lord of Heaven and Earth," suggests the "sky," which suggests the fine day to be thanked for, which suggests the children which brings us back to Sunday School, and the teachers to be prayed for, then the parents, then upstairs in the home where one is sick, then the vacant chair in the home and so on. Sometimes it is a constantly widening circle, beginning with the individual and ending with the world and heaven. Sometimes it is clear that the minister has no idea where he is going, one feels him catch wildly at any straw of suggestion which comes in his way, while his sentences begin as if there was no ending for them in view, and he is constantly remembering certain people or causes omitted in one of his earlier petitions, and going back to make up the deficiency. The imperfectly read prayer owing to the mechanical difficulty of reading without seeming to read, the fawning prayer which makes the hearer feel that the minister cannot believe God to be personal, as no real person could tolerate such flattery, the haphazard repetition by the mouth of stilted conventional phrases used every Sunday—such pulpit prayers give the Catholic priest all the advantage because the onlooker cannot prove so definitely that there is nothing going on in the clergyman's head. In all such cases the state of the clerical mind is apt to be reproduced along lay lines in the congregation. But people can really pray if they want anything badly enough after they have done everything they possibly can do to get it. In such cases prayers are brief, passionate, simple, and definite. The real leader in prayer is one who can shatter the self-satisfaction and comfortableness of a congregation and express for them the sleeping yearnings and hunger of their deeper selves. Some of the collects in the Book of Common Prayer show how this can be done without the use of rhetoric, some of Martineau's prayers produce by rhetorical means similar results. For peace, resignation and quietness the collect form seems most suited. Here is a perfect example:

"O God, who hast prepared for those who love thee such good things as pass man's understanding; pour into our hearts such love toward thee, that we, loving thee above all things, may obtain thy promises, which exceed all that we can desire; through Jesus Christ our Lord. Amen." [1]

This becomes more loved and more effective the oftener it is used or heard. It is bare and simple. But one full of metaphors and pictures may exercise a similar influence on those to whom it has become familiar:

"O Lord, support us all day long of this troublous life, until the shadows lengthen and the evening comes, and the busy world is hushed, and the fever of life is over, and our work is done. Then in Thy mercy grant us a safe lodging, and a holy rest, and peace at the last; through Jesus Christ our Lord. Amen." [2]

But even such miracles of devotional art cannot take the place of a few sentences of personal prayer from the minister himself, fitted to the particular needs of the day, the place and the people, as Father Mapple, before preaching his sermon on Jonah in the belly of the fish, "paused a little; then kneeling in the pulpit bows, folded his large brown hands across his chest, uplifted his closed eyes, and offered a prayer so deeply devout that he seemed kneeling and praying at the bottom of the sea." [8]

The most moving scene for many in all the pageant of Catholicism is when the priest enters the chancel with the censer, and one sees the clouds of fragrant incense rising heavenward, the prayers of the saints. Yes, the picture moves, but it remains after all a dead material symbol, when one compares it with its Protestant counterpart, intellectual, aesthetic, spiritual, a living soul, uniting in its upward flight the souls of a whole congregation.

In order really to appreciate an ordinary church group, a minister should have tasted the atmosphere of other groups organized around other motives. If he had been present at a directors' meeting, intent on profits at any cost, or at some gathering of professional patriots hot with hysteria and hate, or seen the winks of dishonest political compromise go round the board, or sat through sessions of dreary drunkenness, or lectures filled with the sad clarity of pure intellect, he would come back with relief to his own little group of ordinary church folk, with new tenderness and hope. Here at least are people organized not for the purpose of exploiting the weak, nor in order to get drunk periodically, nor to spread suspicion, nor to hide dishonesty by throwing dust in the face of the public, nor to exhibit their own superior sense of despair. He would find the occasion on its knees before him praying for someone adequately to express its normal healthy human quality, and his whole being would burst forth into a song of praise, a public prayer of aspiration, thanksgiving and devotion. For the years have taken away most of the selfish advantages of church-going, and even in the largest congregations, there are some who are hungering and thirsting after righteousness.

It is not a cause for regret when a minister is not equipped with an easy flowing vocabulary. The speaker who is intoxicated with the exuberance of his own verbosity can dream at most of exercising an empty hypnotic power over himself and the other more shallow-pated members of his congregation, his condition is like that of Aubrey in the last audible words of Shaw's play *Too True to be Good:* "And meanwhile my gift has possession of me: I must preach and preach and preach no matter how late the hour and how short the day, no matter whether I have nothing to say——"

A real sermon passes through every part of the man who delivers it. Brain builds its skeleton of thought, passion covers it with warm flesh and blood, experience clothes it in everyday garments, imagination makes it live, body keeps its feet on the ground, originality gives it its own gait, common-sense removes its artificiality, revision straightens its tie. But in delivery it leaves the organism which gave it birth, and begins to live a life of its own, does better things than had been planned, astonishes its parent till he stands in spirit like the hen watching the duck she has hatched out, upon the water she herself would not dare to enter.

After the initial agonies of composition and correction and the nervous fear of failure are over, the delivery of a sermon as one looks back upon it is a great experience. As the brain grows heated, as the self is forgotten, as the congregation respond, a sense of indwelling power and direction makes one for the time being at once the director of a current and a craft navigating on its swiftly flowing surface. The atmosphere becomes electric and the arrows of thought, like Alcestes' arrows, take fire as they fly. A new phrase, better than anything which had been written occurs on the spur of the moment. One hears oneself at times discarding notes and using an illustration, far more felicitous than that which had been designed, to enforce the truth, and at the end of the sentence adding those few touches that come out so unexpectedly and seem more like deeds than words, transforming rhetoric into reality. No one who has ever spoken on occasions of great local or national emergency, exultation or distress, or to great groups of soldiers or sailors about to face fearful odds, can forget how sometimes after the preliminary skirmish to gain and hold distracted attention, the miracle has sometimes happened, and he felt suddenly between the seconds that through him there was passing that current which was glowing incandescent in the brain of every man before him.

There is a subtle intermixture of the mental and emotional processes of a whole congregation, felt by each one not privately but as a sharer in what all are experiencing together. And sometimes it seems for a moment as if something actually takes place as Abt Vogler heard it in his music, heaven yearns down, and touches earth, and all together feel "a flash of the will that can." The benediction is pronounced. The service is over. Looking back for a moment the minister feels that with the experience he now has had, he could write a really great sermon on that text. He would like to do it, but then—there is next Sunday!

But it will be said, this is only one way of composing and delivering a sermon. There are many others. The Reverend Thomas Binney of the King's Weigh House Chapel in London used to tell preachers that all that was necessary was to gather your materials together and then set fire to them in the pulpit. Lord Jeffrey says that Curran whose speeches on behalf of the accused in state trials placed him in the forefront of Irish orators used at first to address the court entirely extempore.[4] "But when his rising reputation made him more chary of his fame, he tried for some time to write down, and commit to memory, the more important parts of his pleadings. The result, however, was not at all encouraging; and he soon laid aside his pen so entirely as scarcely even to make any notes in preparation. He meditated his subjects, however, when strolling in his garden, or more frequently when idling over his violin, and often prepared in this way those splendid passages and groups of images with which he was afterwards to dazzle and enchant his admirers. The only notes he made were often of the metaphors he proposed to employ, and these of the utmost brevity. For the grand peroration, for example, in H. Rowan's case, his notes were as follows: 'Character of Mr. R.: *Furnace—Rebellion—Smothered —Stalks—Redeeming Spirit.*' From such slight hints he spoke fearlessly, and without cause for fear. With the help of such a scanty chart, he plunged boldly into the unbuoyed channel of his cause, and trusted himself to the torrent of his own eloquence, with no better guidance than such landmarks as these. It almost invariably happened that the experiment succeeded, that his own expectations were far exceeded: and that, when his mind came to be more intensely heated by his subject, and by that inspiring confidence which a public audience seldom fails to infuse into all who are sufficiently gifted to receive it, a multitude of new ideas, adding vigor or ornament, were given off; and it also happened that in the same prolific moments, and as their almost inevitable consequence, some crude and fantastic notions escaped, which, if they impeach the author's taste, at least leave him the merit of a splendid fault which none but men of genius can commit."

Rowland Hill felt that initial nervousness and a humble sense of incompetency were a great advantage to a preacher. He said to one young man who had ascended the pulpit with great confidence and had broken down in the middle of his sermon: "Young man, had you ascended the pulpit in the spirit in which you descended, you would have descended in the spirit in which you ascended." But Frederick William Robertson after some of his greatest sermons was known to say to a friend: "Have I made a fool of myself?" The great George Whitefield apparently never knew what it was to prepare a sermon. Usually for an hour or so before he entered the pulpit he used to retire with a few commentaries and Cruden's Concordance. But then it must be remembered that George Whitefield *was* the sermon. He lived always apparently on the high spiritual plane which the ordinary preacher reaches only in moments of rare achievement, and he spoke to congregations who were intensely interested in religion so that before dawn on Sunday mornings "the streets were thronged with people lighting their way by lanterns to hear him."

The fact of course is that all men cannot work the same way. For this reason the Beecher lectures are given by a different man each year. On the face of a watch you have three hands all working differently. It would be a mistake to imagine that the second hand was doing all the work, and the hour hand doing no work at all. Every man has to find his natural tempo. Out of some men there seems to flow naturally and without effort the richest spiritual vocabulary, some men come to the boiling point too soon, before either their own thought or the emotion of their congregations are ready for it; other men can never let themselves go, they simmer but never boil. Like some dancers who cannot yield to the music, but hold themselves stiff and muscle-bound, in position for its sudden stop, so some preachers can never trust themselves to the flow of their thought, to the wave of their inspiration.

The thesis of these lectures is that most men are more apt to be carried away by thought after doing some thinking for themselves; that all except geniuses are more likely to perform the impossible after achieving the possible; that with a modern congregation, the mind and heart must be induced to operate before the soul evolves; that it is the disciplined rather than the undisciplined life which catches impulses from vernal woods, and to which things come of themselves. For the saint, for the genius, the things written here are not necessarily true. These lectures are for ordinary people, they are for sinners only.

It is interesting to study the effect of preaching on

the minister, on the casual attendant, and on the regular congregation.

Every profession, it has been said, is a conspiracy against the laity. On the other hand, it may be said with equal justice, that the laity push young men into the professions, in order that there may be someone to do the things which the laity think ought to be done, but which they do not care to do themselves. Emerson expressed the lay mind in this respect when he confessed:

> I like a church; I like a cowl;
> I love a prophet of the soul;
> And on my heart monastic aisles
> Fall like sweet strains, or pensive smiles;
> Yet not for all his faith can see
> Would I that cowled churchman be.[5]

There seems to be something unnatural in committing a young man for life to certain views, forcing him to defend and talk about them regularly so many times a week. But as has been pointed out before, there is something unnatural about all professional life and the spending of one's time at any job. The traffic policeman, the surgeon, the school teacher, the banker, all are apt to become warped by their jobs. Bernard Shaw has perhaps made the most valiant attempt of any to retain the absolutely lay mind of the child, talking heresy in his plays as soldier or business man, rich man or poor man, doctor, minister, man or woman, without any of the prejudices or superstitions of each group, but even he becomes a professional when he speaks of himself and his own works: "My conscience," he says, "is the genuine pulpit article: it annoys me to see people comfortable when they ought to be uncomfortable; and I insist on making them think in order to bring them to conviction of sin. If you don't like my preaching you must lump it. I really cannot help it." [6] Even he cannot enjoy the privilege of being absolutely lay. But because his professionalism does not fit into any of the established groups a special adjective had to be coined to describe it, the word "Shavian." A minister might just as well admit to himself that he is a professional, there are certain things he must speak of as certainties and treat with reverence, as doctors of vaccination, or lawyers of the rules of cross-examination. A speaker who is sceptical about any possible moral improvement of the race, or the feasibility of a just society, or the existence of unused reservoirs of spiritual power, may be some other kind of professional, but certainly is not a minister. A minister is set apart from other men, just as everyone who is doing anything in the world is set apart from others as he does it. "Please do not talk to the man at the wheel!"

But in every profession there are certain unnecessary and deplorable deformities which are caused by the routine performance of regular duties. It used to be said that any school ma'rm could be recognized as a school ma'rm two blocks off; a successful banker looks at you from behind an invisible brass grille; a doctor cannot altogether divorce himself from his antiseptic bedside manner; while it was said of one elderly minister, "the folds of skin hung loose about a jaw, accustomed to a lifetime's enunciation of platitudes."

It is undoubtedly bad for any man to be permitted to speak for half an hour every week to his fellow men without interruption. It is dangerous for him when the subject is one in which a hallowed haze can be made so easily to cover slovenliness and dishonesty of thought and preparation; pious phrases cover a multitude of sins. It is still more dangerous when he has to speak with emotion, for lofty emotions are apt to leave one with the sense that one has done enough good for the present, and they all bring with them a crowd of relatives who are very near, but not very lofty. There is a curious connection between orthodoxy and meanness; evangelical rapture and financial untrustworthiness; liberalism and bigotry; temperance and gluttony; the expansiveness of the pulpit and the constriction of personal generosity. An expert is "an ordinary man far enough away from home," and a saint's reputation too often depends upon the silence of his family. It is almost fatal to allow a man this freedom of preaching when he knows that there is so little external check upon his activity. When one compares the work of a minister with that of a travelling salesman who has to send in his orders week by week, in the face of fierce competition or lose his position, one appreciates how severe the internal compulsion must be in the man himself if he is to be fired at all times to do the very best work of which he is capable. "The light that convinces of sin is the light that saves," and if a minister is aware of the besetting sins of a preacher, he can avoid them. "Thee o'er thyself, I therefore crown and mitre," said Virgil to the pilgrim as he came to the higher circles of the Purgatorio,[7] thus must the preacher operate as his own task master and his own bishop, if his inner life is to control his circumstances.

One of the great advantages of religious conferences which ministers are expected to attend is that it gives them a chance as members of the audience to make a study of the mental condition of boredom. The preacher can now analyse for once that state from which his congregation suffers so often. He will find that he comforts himself as he takes his place in the pew and reads over the list of addresses on the program, with the thought that up to this point in the history of the world, all public addresses have ultimately come to an end. But then he remembers with horror that this is merely an induction from past facts and provides no assurance that these particular addresses may not go on forever. He discovers that boredom has little to do with the length of the address. A pile of manuscript before the speaker which has to be read attracts the attention of all in the audience. Few speeches are so good as to make the people oblivious of the number of pages still on the unread side. A sensitive listener can feel the rebellion on the part of the people when the speaker says "finally," or "in conclusion," at a time when they can clearly see quite a pile of sheets on the unread side, and the subconscious protest almost boils when with only a few sheets yet to read the speaker does not play fair and begins to turn his papers over, showing that the last are written on both sides. But, in general, the presence of a manuscript is comforting as a pledge of the fact that the address will come to an end sometime. An extempore address when the audience is afflicted with boredom is much more terrible, as a minister said after one such freely flowing affair: "I thought and thought and could discover no reason why the speaker should ever stop at any particular point." Boredom is a condition when the speaker either by his voice or manner does not interest his hearers. The minds of the audience wander, "Is so and so on the platform really as attentive as he appears to be, or has he better control of his facial muscles than I have?" Every detail of the pulpit furniture, of one's own vest, of the hairs on the neck of the man in front I study carefully for the tenth time, a spirit of resignation ensues as the droning proceeds, then rebellion as I find it impossible to follow my own train of thought, since isolated words of the speaker interfere with their own suggestions. "Why did I ever come here? How dry my eye-balls are! Yet if I shut them people will think I am asleep!" the sense of being caught in an uninteresting and boring situation in the midst of an interesting and inviting world overwhelms one. At last the voice ceases and I look at my watch. Eighty-five minutes instead of the forty minutes allotted to him! and I join in the perfunctory applause, visibly, but taking care not to add perceptibly to the sound.

Pure boredom from which the human race has suf-

fered so interminably in school, at church, on festivals
and anniversaries, might be symbolized by a picture
in which people are seen sitting in rows as the occasion requires, but someone has built up a brick wall
separating the platform from the body of the house,
someone has forgotten to turn on the heat and the
light. The people sit in rows staring in the dark at
the cold brick wall. They are bored. They owe it to
their social position to be there. The occasion is on its
knees praying for someone to express it for those who
have come together. But the speaker is engaged in sav
ing his own soul, satisfied with the ritual of a prepared
paper which says all the expected things, or a plea for
further funds, or he is meandering extemporaneously
producing used objects from the dusty lumber-room
of his own mind.

Let the listening preacher as he sits meditate upon
the question: "What would save this terrible situation?" It is clear to him that what is needed is an oasis
in the desert, a few simple sincere characteristic words
breaking into the uniformity of the paper, a change in
the tone of the voice impelled by a new vision in the
imagination of the speaker, a boiling down, and compression in the verbiage, impelled by a desire to stop
talking and say something, a sudden union between a
living imagination and the awakened spirits of the
congregation. A new speaker arises and lo! all separa-
tion between the platform and floor of the house disappears, all within those walls are now one, seeing the
pictures, thinking the thoughts in the inner living of
one whose voice has in it the music of his thought.

They forget entirely where they are or how long they have been there, and as they think of his address afterwards it seems to them to have about it the beauty of a personal relation which however brief in time, in eternity is everlasting.

The good results of preaching on the preacher may be summed up briefly in the fact that the sacred things which it is his duty continually to handle for his daily bread do not become common or unclean to him from his constant familiarity with them, but grow in wonder and loveliness with his growing experience of them, and that sometimes in the midst of the strain of the week's work he hears a voice from his own pulpit of last Sunday expressing a gospel for his needs, and is constrained, perhaps only tentatively and afar off, yet humbly and sincerely, "to folwe it himself." It is hard to say whether good preachers have been equally distinguished as good men, perhaps the very nervous constitution and critical insight of the preacher make it more difficult for him than for others; some of them seem to have put all they had into their sermons and to have had little left over for the rough and tumble of ordinary life where they are not on an elevated structure above their fellows. Almost all ministers' wives dream of a time when their husbands could be free simply to preach and be released from all the other harassing pastoral and personal duties, in their great charity they realize that their husbands are after all best in the pulpit. But Chaucer's ideal holds, in some arts it may be true that you can teach people how to do something without

being able to do it yourself, but this is not true of the
art of living. The gibe that those who can, do; those
who can't, teach; and those who can neither do nor
teach, teach how to teach is of doubtful validity anywhere, but is the most dangerous heresy in a region
where it is so easy to mistake a good vocabulary for
a good life.

The effect of preaching upon the casual attendant
is of some importance to the growth of a preacher's
congregation and his success as a speaker to other
groups. The regular congregation come to church in
a prepared mood. They know the preacher, and much
of the interest arises from the fact that it is he who is
saying these things. The presence of the casual listener
is an antiseptic influence arresting the morbid development of a private-chaplain type of sentimental personality. The stranger must be caught and held more
objectively by the content of the sermon. When one
knows someone intimately one allows for certain ex-
aggerations and eccentricities and is interested in personal side-lights, which might repel a stranger. It is
often hard for parish ministers to hold the attention
of college audiences. They feel the lack of a congregation which is personally friendly and intimate. They
have nothing to depend upon but the value of their
message. No one is going home delighted to tell
friends of the cute incident which Mr. Blank related
in the sermon about his little Alice, but he faces a critical group who are not much interested in him and
are slightly sceptical about what he can give them.

The atmosphere for the college preacher differs

according to whether attendance is voluntary or required. Under the former system the preacher speaks to the few already interested in formal religion, under the latter system he addresses many who are entirely indifferent and uninterested. A secularizing group which has no roots in the soil and no appreciation of the foundations and historical traditions of American colleges insists that religion is a subject like stamp-collecting, which interests some and not others, and that the attempt to bring all students into touch with the traditions of college chapel only leads to hypocrisy and disgust. A noble band of religious liberals hold a theory of the matter illustrated by the remark which Dr. Charles W. Eliot is reported to have made to one who alleged that required religion at college was better than no religion at all: "My mind is not subtle enough to catch the distinction," they apply this theory to religion, but curiously enough not to art or literature or science. There are still some who feel that while purely voluntary services can operate in large universities and in colleges located in cities, the choice in the case of smaller colleges more remotely situated is between some form of compulsion and the total abandonment of all formal religious exercises. This does not mean that the appeal of religion is weaker than that of art, literature or any other cultural interest, but that in an atmosphere where so much is required by public opinion and examination, that which can be for the present neglected is neglected. The compulsion implied in the case of other subjects by the presence of tests in the background seems inapplicable where religion is concerned, yet it seems hardly fair to allow the somewhat unnatural atmosphere generated in an insulated group of adolescents to develop without any of the influences of religious services. The loss to such a group is similar to that sustained by a neighborhood of city children who have never seen the country. The "visiting preacher" method of bringing religion before the student body by the best experts available may not be the best way, but up to the present no better plan has been discovered. The ideal state would be one in which there were no taxes but everyone contributed voluntarily to the limit of his ability, the ideal college would be one where there were no examinations or compulsions, but for the present the pure essence of liberty seems to need a container formed of necessity if it is not to seep away into abject slavery to natural sloth and easy-going public opinion. It is for the people to decide whether in this somewhat arid era all formal religion should be banished from the colleges until the poetry of its presence is again appreciated and desired.

A study of the effect of preaching on the regular congregation can only be made by self-examination, and much resented questioning of habitual churchgoers. A preacher's opinion on the subject undergoes a change when he becomes a hearer rather than a speaker at church. His dominant feeling had been that of disappointment at small congregations, but now is

one of astonishment that so many people still come
to church. When he tries to discover what effect, if
any, preaching has upon himself and others, he discovers that no long ingrained habit, no sense of social
duty, no desire to show himself friendly could force
him to attend regularly some churches or listen to
some ministers. He finds that nearly all the old primitive reasons for church-going are invalid in his case.
When he questions other people he finds that there
are still many motives at work, but that at the core of
most of them there is something worthy. Habit, the
opinion of the neighbors, the influence on or of the
children, contacts of value in business and professional
life, all play their part. But all of these are insufficient
to force an intelligent man today to attend church
regularly unless he finds it to be of value to his own
inner life. The sermon still is felt to be of value by
many common, ordinary folk who have not much
opportunity for reflective thought, and also by some
of the finer and more thoughtful members of any
community. The middle group of smoother, more
sophisticated, less thoughtful, more self-satisfied people who live on the surface of life find little to interest them in sermons or indeed in religion.

There seem to be religious periods and veins in human lives. For very few is it uniformly religious.
There are certain types of people to whom religion
will never mean very much, and the attempt to stretch
the meaning of the word to cover everything of human interest is probably futile, as in this very incorrectly quoted verse from a popular rhyme:

> Straight from the tee the ball in one
> Was cupped in velvet sod,
> Some call it mighty lucky golf,
> And others call it God.

It is better to admit that only some people and these only at certain times are religious. There is a time for everything even religion, and the attempt to produce this time on regular schedule can never be wholly successful. An unconscious humorist once said: "Evening services can only be made successful if they are held every Sunday night or not at all." But he was wrong even in that which he was trying to say. There is wisdom in the Catholic practice of special times and seasons. There are occasions when the thought and emotion of a whole community can be aroused to deeper experience. Every church might well be open fifty-two Sundays in the year, but in almost every church there are certain periods of the year when it might be prepared as a quiet spot for prayer, and people permitted to realize that the text does not read, "Where a sermon is preached to two or three in my name, there am I in the midst of them." Religion should be a continuous background, a pervading spirit in a life, but its expression might sometimes be made more living if it were not assumed to be so uniformly regular. It is hard to convince the modern man that listening to a sermon every week is a duty he owes to God.

When one compares the effect of a church service and especially of a sermon upon oneself as compared to that made by a play, a film or a concert, one must

555555555

confess that very seldom does the influence of the sermon seem to be as strong or as permanent. The moral and spiritual change wrought upon people by dramatic representation, and by music seem more worth while than anything which can be attempted by the average church service and sermon. When a really great spirit either as author or composer or actor or performer uses these other media, he seems to have at his disposal resources immensely greater than can be commanded by a simple church outfit of pulpit, organ and choir. Competition seems almost out of the question, and some churches are tempted to make use of these other media in a kind of second-hand manner. As one London preacher once said of another, "It is easy to fill your church if you have the band of the Gordon Highlanders in the choir seats." Nothing attracts the floating public like the novelty of using an equipment for a purpose for which it was not meant, nothing could exceed their multitudinous delight if they could see Barnum and Bailey's circus in a Cathedral Chancel. But if the preacher is determined to use his historic edifice for the purpose of worship and religious inspiration only, there are some considerations which are worth his attention. It is evident that a great deal of the weakness of the church is due to its habit of depending upon a kind of superstitious special privilege. Artists who use the other media mentioned know that they can depend upon nothing but their own skill and hard work, an infinite attention to details, the drudgery of sustained effort and merciless practice and revision. The minister on the other hand is inclined to depend upon the habit and custom of his congregation, and on a certain identification of his own services with people's duty towards God. There is no special privilege in the service of God. Ordination does not set one apart from the regular disciplines of life. Some of the writers of the worst hymns and the most saccharine tunes were undoubtedly desirous of serving God, but they failed to do so. There is no magic about being a minister. All servants of God operate under the same dispensation. All art is the characteristic use of certain tools and materials. There is no formula which makes truth and efficiency any more easy to reach in the sphere of religion than in the sciences and the arts. Putting a spire on a house and dedicating it to God does not make it immune from the infinite and meticulous care and labor which is necessary in the framing of any other instrument designed for some valuable purpose.

There is also much comfort for the minister in the fact that in spite of all competition there is an essen-tial element in preaching which is not found in the same degree in any of the other arts. Everywhere else what is said has to be taken with a discount, with the remembrance that it does not count at its face value because the author is speaking through a character in a play or in a novel, or the speaker is running for office, or is advertising a special product, or represents a special interest, or is giving the public what they think they want. The tradition of preaching is that here a man is speaking without fear or favor. There is a sound about the best preaching that differs from any of the sounds of the world. It deals with the most pressing problems of life and yet is disinterested, it is like a voice of God amid the insistent clamor of special interests. All through human history attempts have been made to control the pulpit, with more or less success. But its professional ethics have always clearly insisted upon its freedom. It is no new thing that the world should be annoyed because the pulpit does not play its game. The report of the parliamentary committee on the decay of trade made in Great Britain in 1669 advised that "some ease and relaxation in ecclesiastical matters" would be "a means of improving the trade of this Kingdom," [8] and this desire of men of affairs for "some ease and relaxation," has remained up to the present day in their feeling that Micah is of no great help to the armament industry, and that Amos did not look at matters either from the point of view of a deacon or a shareholder, and that in general "they didn't know everythin' down in Judee." [9] Sometimes the church has capitulated as in most wars, and in occasional cases of ministers, speculating in the stockmarket, who preached during the textile strikes in New England sermons on such texts as "My Father worketh hitherto and I work," proving thereby that Christ was in favor of long hours, low wages and large dividends in textile mills. But still in spite of many ignoble capitulations and much too tactful silence, the tradition of freedom has been practiced and does remain.

When one compares the appeal made by an ordinary sermon with the impression produced by a play, or a ritualistic service well performed, one understands what the Roman Catholic priest meant when he said, "In your Protestant churches you read to them out of a cook-book, in our Catholic churches we give them a meal." One has the same feeling when one sees a play like "Dead End," and compares the effect upon the audience in enlightening and rationalizing their attitude toward social justice, with the impressions made by a sermon designed to produce the same effects. The sympathy for people who used to be so often described in prayer-meetings as "those less fortunate than ourselves," the rebellion against the waste of fine human material by a social system which is so careful of dead property and so careless of living beings, the conviction of the ugliness of vice and crime, such a play brings home these impressions to the audience in a more permanent and real manner, we are inclined to think, than can be done in any sermon. The reason is that most sermons are abstractions. They do not attempt to picture life as it is with all its irrelevance, its vagrant humor, its non-moral roughage, its imperfections and inexplicabilities. The sermon abstracts from life its moral lessons, its religious strand, its rationale, its more exalted moods, and strives to present them alone as the essentials of living. All abstraction tends to become unreal, unfair and uninteresting. It is much easier for the minister to stand up in the pulpit and say, "If you love God, nothing else matters," than it is for the playwright, keeping close to life, to show his audience that in spite of everything, something like that might really be true. The playwright seems to do it better because he does not seem to the audience to set out to do it. He seems to be trying to give you a fair picture of life, and it is life itself rather than the author which seems to imply that selfishness and vice are ugly and virtue and human kindness are lovely. The interest of the congregation is dampened by the conviction that the minister is committed to his conclusion before he starts. At a certain theological seminary the professor of apologetics announced that next day he would discuss the question of the existence of God without any presuppositions whatsoever, he said he would start fairly without prejudging the issue and see how far he and his class would be able to go in the matter. Next day when they were met together he started by saying: "This is a solemn task on which we are engaged to-day, and I think we could not do better than opening our session by asking God's blessing upon our under-taking, let us join in prayer!" For a philosopher such an order of events might be justified, but not to a con-gregation of modern ordinary folk.

In spite of all this the sermon still has its place and its power. Especially in a world where so many plays and novels are composed for the purpose of emphasiz-ing the sordid and hopeless nature of life, and the futil-ity of virtue. But the preacher must take in the sweep of the scythe a much broader swath of reality than has been customary in the past. His convictions must appear to his congregation to be built out of the tex-ture of reality. His task is to throw light upon life as they know it inside and outside themselves, complicating for them their simple material prejudices by considerations of which they had not thought, simplifying for them their doubts and fears by confession of their universality and mystery and often of their unreality. The sermon is particularly fitted to express the larger, longer views of life, the vision from the mountain top which is a part of everyman's property. But in order to do so fittingly, it is necessary for the minister to know and to love life in all its phases. He can only tempt people over the fairy bridge of faith into lands unknown when he has gained their confidence by the wonders which he has shown their in their own back yards and common streets. He must be a bit of a poet before he can become a reputable prophet, and this is what Rupert Brooke says about how it feels to be a poet:

"It consists in just looking at people and things as themselves—neither as useful nor moral nor ugly nor anything else; but just as being. At least that's a philosophical description of it. What happens is that I suddenly feel the extraordinary value and importance of everything I meet, and almost everything I see. . . . I roam about places—yesterday I did it even in Birmingham!—and sit in trains and see the essential glory and beauty of all the people I meet. I can watch a dirty middle-aged tradesman in a railway-carriage for hours, and love every dirty greasy sulky wrinkle in his weak chin and every button on his spotted unclean waistcoat. I know their states of mind are bad. But I'm so much occupied with their being there at all, that I don't have time to think of that. I tell you that a Birmingham gouty Tariff Reform fifth-rate business man is splendid and immortal and desirable." [10]

When a real human being with such a touch of the poetic in him has also experienced that kind of cosmic vision which is religion, then you have the proper foundation for a preacher who can lead people through the wonders of their own immediate environment to become conscious of one which is greater.

Ministers, perhaps more than any other profession, have insisted upon quarrelling with their bread and butter. It is this tradition of disinterestedness which gives reality to preaching over any of the other arts. At its highest, art ceases to be art and becomes life. It ceases to pose and begins to live. The shape of a chunk of marble suggests to Michael Angelo a figure which might be made out of it. His work seems to him to be releasing that figure from the superfluous matter which surrounds it. At last his human figure is completed, the final chip of encasing matter in which it was buried has been removed. It stands there perfect and almost living, but not quite, that is as far as sculpture goes. The miracle of Pygmalion has never been performed. But real preaching must take that next step. Submitting to all the disciplines of inspiration, vision, the infinite capacity for taking pains, close observation, tireless experiment, hard-won skill, it must further perform the impossible miracle of making the dead bones live. Art at its highest comes to a point where there is nothing further to be done except for everything to live. "Why don't they march?" asked

the small boy, looking at the soldiers on the Shaw
monument on Boston Common. The preacher's work
of art must sink itself into the stream of life, begin to
move as a part of it, dissolved into its current. The
sermon must be something taken along with him in the
swing of his ordinary living.

What is the effect of such preaching on the regular
congregation? Here one may speak for oneself. Any
man who was a student in Edinburgh thirty-five years
ago knows that the preachers of that day changed
his life. The whole course of his inner thought and
feeling was deepened and directed by the great souls
who spoke from those pulpits. Then, at Free St.
Georges, Alexander White, an old man, with his stern
and lofty view of God's majesty, was said to blacken
the saints in the morning, while Hugh Black, a young
man, with his human sympathy whitened the sinners
in the evening, then John Kelman seemed to be burning himself out like a coal from the very altar of God
as he gave himself to his great congregation of students. Rabbi A. B. Davidson would not preach in pulpits, but his class room became a sanctuary for his
students, when at times the exact scholar prophesied
before them, for though most of his time was spent
upon the details of the grammar and syntax of Arabic
and Hebrew, yet on rare and splendid occasions he
used to wrap his robes around him and speak, as one
inspired, to his students of the greatness of their calling in meeting the individual man, "If you could appear before him," he would say, "as the apostolic men
appeared in the world, with the awe upon them of a

glorious presence which they had just left, and a fellowship, ceased in the flesh, yet forever unbroken; with the fire of a new life within them fusing all their faculties, and giving them a flexibility more than that of men; laden with a few great ideas which they presented in every manner, to every man's conscience," or he would pause in his exegesis of a passage from one of the prophets to urge upon his Calvinistically systematized students a more human appreciation of the life of Christ, "He took away the world's sin by making the world feel it was not all sinful. . . . His life broke in upon the weary, monotonous universality and hopelessness of sin." [11]

All sermons then were written, but as one looks back upon that experience one finds that it was not the scheme or the subject of any sermon, but that it is some spark hit off almost incidentally from the anvil of the preacher's mind in the course of developing his thesis, which still glows in one's own mind, actively contributing to one's own life.

What has been, can be. It is a comfort to think that the people who have stopped going to church, and go each week the same number of times now to the movies with dreary uniformity, did not get out of those visits to church any more than they now get out of the movies. They want a comfortable habit, giving them a sense of having somewhere to go in their free time, they want diversion, escape for an hour from lives that lead nowhere, and there were many in the congregations of the past who got just these things and no more from habitual church-going. When the spectator sees in his own generation the escape from the one bad habit of deadly automatic church-going into its modern form of deadly habitual automatic movie-going, interspersed with quick auto trips to road houses "where you get a wonderful meal," he is apt to react as that astute commentator on modern life, Mr. T. S. Eliot does, and ejaculate:

> Wipe your hand across your mouth, and laugh;
> The worlds revolve like ancient women
> Gathering fuel in vacant lots.[12]

The change in popular habits about church-going is less important than it seems. The old women have simply shifted to another vacant lot. But today a man who has a burning message to deliver, and has disciplined himself into the ability to deliver it, and who has thrust his roots deep down into the rich mulch of history and tradition, cannot be hidden. He is more in demand than ever before, because people possess more things to be discontented about than ever before, his congregation will have selected itself more rationally than the congregation of the past. As one minister, the son of a minister, said to his father, "the difference between the congregation you used to have and mine is this—if any member of your parish was absent from church there was a reason; if any member of my parish is present at church, there is a reason." This condition is satisfactory. He desires no special privilege such as a private wire to the Almighty about the next world used to give to the priest. He is a human being who if he can be the medium of bringing to others something which is real and valuable will in the end discover a demand greater than he can supply. He still is the means of changing lives.

These lectures began with the first search by the preacher for an idea to preach about. They have followed the birth and development of that idea in his mind, his attempt to express it to himself, to write and revise it for his people, to deliver it to his congregation. They have studied the effects of his preaching on himself, his regular congregation and casual attendants. In a famous French novel M. Jules Romains pictures the secondary individual existence of a solitary engineer which begins at the moment of his death. The author continues the story down to the point, months later, when the last man ever to remember is touched by the last faint eddy made on human consciousness by the existence and death of that engineer.[13] So the story of the inception, incubation, and delivery of a sermon should be brought to its fitting conclusion. The stone was dropped into the pool of life. Circles begin to eddy out from that center, touching the walls of the church, the dinner-tables of the parish, the lives of Monday and perhaps Tuesday, till the very last faint vibration caused by that utterance dies away. A Welsh miner said on coming out of church after an eloquent spiritual sermon: "Oh, it would have been wonderful if only he had sung the conclusion!" The conclusion of a true sermon should continue singing itself in the lives of the congregation. An old man once said that in his youth he had heard Jenny Lind singing "I know that my Redeemer liveth," and that the certainty and blessedness of that "know" had continued to sing in his life ever since. The writer never heard Jenny Lind, but that old man passed on to him something which continues to sing in his life, and the voice is hers. Many a sermon not known to print lives on like such a song in lives which have heard it or heard about it. Robertson, Beecher, Spurgeon, Brooks, Bushnell—it is not really their printed sermons that survive, as you will know if you have ever met and talked with some understanding and remembering soul who heard them.

Some sermons miss being literature because they are too poor, others because they are too good. They are more a part of life than of literature. The word becomes flesh and dwells among us. Preaching does not survive, because it goes into solution in life. Life was not given to us that we might be religious, but religion was given to us that we might live. It is good to think of a real sermon as the water in a saucer placed in a hot, dry room, which entirely disappears during the week because the room needs it. Other art is done up in a napkin that it may be preserved; it is the record of a particularly fine moment of human experience. This art cannot live except it die and come to life in other lives. It would seem impossible to trace the secondary life of a sermon in the lives of those who were touched by it. Surface indications would sometimes lead one to the pessimistic conclusion that a sermon has as little effect upon a community as an editorial in a daily newspaper. Again and again one has found almost the entire press in New York City upon one side in a municipal election, and at the close of weeks of editorial propaganda, it is found at election that an enormous majority of their readers vote the other way. But the process of education is slow, and with human society it is impossible to make experiments except upon the stage to show what would have happened if one element had been withdrawn from the situation. In spite of the absence of miracles and the presence of surface indications the effects of a sermon on the lives of those who were touched by it is incalculable but tremendous. One cannot even fathom it in one's own personal experience. Truth when brought to one's attention by someone whom one respects in an atmosphere of exaltation and devotion does "sink in." It is impossible to do as Romains attempted to do with his engineer, it is impossible to show the last impression made upon the last man who faintly remembered that sermon, because in such matters of the spirit the effects have no end. Even on the by-ways of heaven the true preacher will be meeting at times those on whose lives long ago the light of heaven shined in his old church, and he will wonder "How did I know about it then?"

NOTES AND REFERENCES

CHAPTER I

Page 2   1. Pope: *An Epitaph intended for Sir Isaac Newton, Works*, Vol. IV, p. 390 (London, 1882).

7   2. Rev. Dr. Büchsel: *My Ministerial Experiences*, p. 31 (London, 1863).

9   3. Friedrich Nietzsche: *Ecce Homo, N's Werke*, Vol. XV, p. 90 (Leipzig, 1912).

10   4. Walt Whitman: Preface to *Leaves of Grass* (1855).

11   5. Phillips Brooks: *The Mystery of Iniquity* (London, 1893), p. 153.

12   6. *The Note Books of Samuel Butler*, p. 105 (London, 1912).

12   7. Walter Pater: *Marius the Epicurean*, Chapter 1.

17   8. J. L. LeB. Hammond: *Town Labourer* (1932), p. 57.

17   9. Frederic Harrison: *The Meaning of History*, p. 6.

18   10. Lord Acton: *Lectures on Modern History*, pp. 316, 318.

19   11. *American Historical Review*, Vol. XL, No. 2, January 1935. Review of the Conclusions of the Commission by Professor John S. Brubacher.

19   12. Charles Dickens: *Hard Times*, Book I, Chapter 16.

20   13. *Savile Correspondence*, p. 173.

24   14. Dante: *Inferno*, Canto V, lines 112-114.

CHAPTER II

Page 26   1. J. Middleton Murry: *The Problem of Style*, p. 78 (Oxford, 1922).

27   2. Plato: *Symposium*, 175e

28   3. R. M. Rilke: *Auguste Rodin,* pp. 53, 54 (Leipzig, 1930).

30   4. Vernon Lee: *The Handling of Words,* pp. 35-41 (London, 1923).

32   5. George Meredith: *Diana of the Crossways,* Chapter 1, p. 11.

39   6. A. N. Whitehead: *Religion in the Making,* p. 23 (New York, 1926).

40   7. Gerald Vann: *On Being Human,* p. 36 (London, 1934).

41   8. E. R. and J. Pennell: *The Life of James McNeill Whistler,* Vol. I, p. 236 (Philadelphia, 1908).

42   9. "Holiness is loveliness of the spirit." Eric Gill.

43   10. Stuart J. Reid: *The Life and Times of Sydney Smith,* p. 67 (London, 1896).

44   11. J. Dover Wilson: *The Essential Shakespeare,* p. 145.

45   12. William Wordsworth: *Lines Composed above Tintern Abbey.*

46   13. Boswell's *Johnson* for the year 1778.

47   14. John Tillotson: *A Sermon Preached at Cripple Gate,* pp. 17, 18 (London, 1709).

47   15. Theodor Gomperz: *Greek Thinkers,* Book III, Chapter 1, p. 314 (New York, 1901).

50   16. George Bernard Shaw: *Major Barbara,* p. 177 (New York, 1910).

52   17. William Roper: *The Mirrour of Vertue in Worldly Greatnes,* pp. 95-98.

CHAPTER III

Page 56   1. Henry Fielding: *Joseph Andrews,* Book II, Chapter 8.

58   2. Joseph Addison: *The Spectator,* Nos. 106, 112.

59   3. Wesley's *Journal,* September 27, 1749.

60   4. F. W. H. Myers: *Saint Paul,* p. 34 (London, 1894). By permission of The Macmillan Company, publishers.

61   5. W. M. Thackeray: *Esmond,* Book II, Chapter 6.

61   6. Rudyard Kipling: *Rewards and Fairies,* p. 225 (New York, 1910).

62 7. Walter Scott: *The Lay of the Last Minstrel*, Canto VI, XXX.

63 8. Ernest Dowson: *Poems*, p. 21 (London, 1922). By permission of Dodd, Mead & Company, publishers.

64 9. Robert Browning: *Christmas Eve*. By permission of The Macmillan Company, publishers.

64 10. *Lux Mundi*, pp. 315-317 (London, 1889).

64 11. For Rev. Mr. Chadband, see Charles Dickens: *Bleak House*, Chapters 19 and 25.

65 12. Lyof Tolstoy: *Resurrection*, Chapters 39, 40.

65 13. Aldous Huxley: *Crome Yellow*, pp. 8off, 179ff (New York, 1921).

65 14. Edith Sichel, see London: *Spectator:* December 1, 1917.

65 15. For the extraordinary influence of the sermon on the English life of the Victorian age, see Amy Cruse: *The Victorians and their Books and Letters*, Chapters 4, 5, 6 (London, 1935). P. H. Ditchfield: *The Old-Time Parson*, Chapter 13 (London, 1908).

66 16. Mary Cholmondeley: *Red Pottage*, Chapter 24. By permission of Edward Arnold & Company, publishers.

67 17. William Dean Howells: *Annie Kilburn*, Chapter 22. Copyright 1888 by Harper & Brothers. Copyright 1915 by W. D. Howells.

67 18. Harriet Beecher Stowe: *Poganuc People*, Chapter 7.

68 19. Abbott and Campbell: *Life and Letters of Benjamin Jowett*, Vol. I, p. 272.

68 20. Herman Melville: *Moby Dick*, Chapter 8.

69 21. T. S. Eliot: *Murder in the Cathedral*. By permission of Harcourt, Brace and Company, publishers.

70 22. Edward Carpenter: *Towards Democracy*, p. 112 (London, 1909). By permission of Albert & Charles Boni, Inc., publishers.

71 23. George Herbert: *A Priest to the Temple*, Chapter 8.

73 24. *Register of John de Grandisson*, ed. Hingeston-Randolph, p. 586.

75   25. Don Marquis: *Chapters for the Orthodox*, pp.
          53-59.
75   26. Boswell's *Johnson* for the year 1763.
76   27. Emerson's *Journals*, April 1, 1838.
76   28. Thoreau's *Journals*, November 16, 1858.
77   29. G. R. Owst: *Preaching in Medieval England*, pp.
          203-205. By permission of The Macmillan Com-
          pany, publishers.
78   30. John Keats: *The Eve of Saint Mark*.
78   31. Edith Gittings Reid: *Woodrow Wilson*, pp. 91, 92
          (New York, 1934).
78   32. Other poems and passages which should have a
          place in such an anthology include James Russell
          Lowell's "The Church," Hawthorne's "The Gen-
          tle Boy" in *Twice-Told Tales*, Shaw's "On Go-
          ing to Church," *The Education of Henry Adams*,
          p. 34.
79   33. "Sermons in stones" and "pulpiteer" in *As You Like
          It* have no authority as legitimate references to
          church affairs. The nearest approach is probably
          the form of "sentences," the medieval form of
          homily in which Friar Lawrence counsels Romeo.
79   34. William Watson: *New Poems*, p. 80.
80   35. Literary Supplement of the *London Times*, Octo-
          ber 30, 1919. By permission of *The Times*.

Chapter IV

Page 84   1. James Melville: *Memoirs*, p. 75.
     86   2. Alexander White: *Newman*, pp. 43, 44. By permis-
             sion of Longmans, Green & Company, publishers.
     86   3. George Herbert: *The Temple*, I, 72.
     89   4. Plinius Secundus: *Epist.* 12 lib. 1.
     90   5. For R. Caracciolo, see Francesco Torraca: Scritti
             Critici (I), (Napoli, 1907).
     96   6. William Wordsworth: Preface to *Lyrical Ballads*
             (1880).
     97   7. Jacques Lefèvre d'Etaples: French New Testament
             (introduction). (1523.)

97   8. Mrs. Humphrey Ward: *A Writer's Recollections,* Vol. I, p. 163.

97   9. James Moffatt: *A New Translation of the New Testament.*

97   10. For a fine discussion of the authorized and revised translations of the Bible, see Robert Bridges: *Collected Essays,* XVI.

99   11. A. C. Bradley: *A Miscellany,* pp. 225, 227, 233.

100   12. J. W. Beach: *The Outlook for American Prose,* p. 23.

100   13. Logan Pearsall Smith: *Trivia,* p. 26 (New York, 1917).

100   14. H. W. Fowler: *A Dictionary of Modern English Usage* (Oxford, 1927), under "Hackneyed Phrases," "Cliché," "French Words," see also James Russell Lowell: *The Biglow Papers,* Introduction, for a list of "old style" and "new style."

103   15. J. H. Newman: *Rise and Progress of Universities,* Chapter 2. By permission of Longmans, Green & Company, publishers.

Chapter V

Page 109   1. Julien Benda: *La Trahison des Clercs,* Chapter 4, pp. 22off.

111   2. Adolf Hitler: *Mein Kampf,* Vol. II, pp. 525, 6.–530, 4, 6.

112   3. A. N. Whitehead: *Process and Reality,* pp. 523, 526.

112   4. J. M. Bird: *Einstein's Theories of Relativity and Gravitation,* Chapter by E. T. Bell.

117   5. Friedrich Nietzsche: *Jenseits von Gut und Böse,* N's *Werke,* Vol. VII, p. 274 (Leipzig, 1923). Oliver Wendell Holmes has expressed more prosaically a similar idea:

> Our whitest pearl we never find,
>   Our ripest fruit we never reach;
> The flowering moments of the mind
>   Lose half their petals in our speech.

And Mr. Ernest Weekley remarks succinctly: "The word has always lagged behind the idea."

117 6. Robert Bridges: *Collected Papers*, VI, p. 209.
119 7. Emile Faguet: *Flaubert*. Eng. Trans., p. 184.
121 8. John Bunyan: *The Pilgrim's Progress*, The Tenth Stage.
122 9. *The Note Books of Samuel Butler*, p. 101 (London, 1912).
122 10. Charles Mauron: *Aesthetics and Psychology*, Eng. Trans., p. 50 (Hogarth Press, London).
125 11. Friedrich Heiler: *Das Gebet*, pp. 410ff (München, 1923).
126 12. G. R. Owst: *Preaching in Medieval England*, p. 237.
126 13. Dictionary of National Biography under 'Maidston, R.'
133 14. Lewis Mumford: "Toward an Organic Humanism," in *The Critique of Humanism*, edited by C. Hartley Grattan, p. 352.
134 15. See for instance R. M. Rilke's poem: *Das Jüngste Gericht*, and *Das Studen-Buch vom Mönchischen Leben*.

CHAPTER VI

Page 138 1. Collect for the Sixth Sunday after Trinity.
139 2. *The Book of Common Prayer*, p. 571 (New York, 1929).
139 3. Herman Melville: *Moby Dick*, Chapter 9.
143 4. Francis Jeffrey: *Contributions to the Edinburgh Review*, Vol. IV, pp. 444, 445.
146 5. Ralph Waldo Emerson: *The Problem*.
147 6. George Bernard Shaw: *Man and Superman*, Introduction, p. 7.
149 7. Dante: Purgatorio, Canto XXVII, line 142.
160 8. G. N. Clark: *The Later Stuarts*, p. 34.
160 9. James Russell Lowell: *The Biglow Papers*, No. III.
164 10. Rupert Brooke: *Memoirs*, I, p. LIII. By permission of Dodd, Mead & Company, publishers.
166 11. A. B. Davidson: *Biblical and Literary Essays*, pp. 299, 294.
167 12. T. S. Eliot: *Preludes* IV. By permission of Harcourt, Brace and Company, publishers.
168 13. Jules Romains: *Mort de Quelqu'un*.

LYMAN BEECHER LECTURES ON PREACHING
YALE UNIVERSITY

ESTABLISHED MAY 2, 1872

1871–74 Henry Ward Beecher, Brooklyn, New York. Yale Lectures on Preaching.

1874–75 John Hall, New York City. God's Word Through Preaching.

1875–76 William M. Taylor, New York City. The Ministry of the Word.

1876–77 Phillips Brooks, Boston, Massachusetts. Lectures on Preaching.

1877–78 R. W. Dale, Birmingham, England. Nine Lectures on Preaching.

1878–79 Matthew Simpson, Philadelphia, Pennsylvania. Lectures on Preaching.

1879–80 Howard Crosby, New York City. The Christian Preacher.

1880–81 J. T. Duryea, Boston, Massachusetts; and others.

1881–82 E. G. Robinson, Providence, Rhode Island. Lectures on Preaching.

1883–84 Nathaniel J. Burton, Hartford, Connecticut. In Pulpit and Parish.

1884–85 Richard S. Storrs, Brooklyn, New York. The American Scholar.

1885–86 William M. Taylor, New York City. The Scottish Pulpit.

1886–87 Washington Gladden, Columbus, Ohio. Tools and the Man.

1887–88   Henry Clay Trumbull, Philadelphia, Pennsylvania. The Sunday School.

1888–89   J. A. Broadus, Louisville, Kentucky. Preaching and the Ministerial Life.

1889–90   A. J. F. Behrends, Brooklyn, New York. The Philosophy of Preaching.

1890–91   James Stalker, Glasgow, Scotland. The Preacher and His Models.

1891–92   A. M. Fairbairn, Oxford, England. The Place of Christ in Modern Theology.

1892–93   Robert F. Horton, London, England. Verbum Dei.

1894–95   David H. Greer, New York City. The Preacher and His Place.

1895–96   Henry Van Dyke, New York City. The Gospel for an Age of Doubt.

1896–97   John Watson, Liverpool, England. The Cure of Souls.

1897–98   W. J. Tucker, Hanover, New Hampshire. The Making and the Unmaking of the Preacher.

1898–99   George Adam Smith, Glasgow, Scotland. Modern Criticism and the Old Testament.

1899–00   John Brown, Bedford, England. Puritan Preaching in England.

1901–02   Washington Gladden, Columbus, Ohio. Social Salvation.

1902–03   George A. Gordon, Boston, Massachusetts. Ultimate Conceptions of Faith.

1903–04   Lyman Abbott, New York City. The Christian Ministry.

1904–05   Francis G. Peabody, Cambridge, Massachusetts. Jesus Christ and the Christian Character.

1905–06   Charles R. Brown, Oakland, California. The Social Message of the Modern Pulpit.

1906–07   P. T. Forsyth, London, England. Positive Preaching and the Modern Mind.

1907–08 William Herbert Perry Faunce, Providence, Rhode Island. The Educational Ideal in the Ministry.

1908–09 H. Hensley Henson, London, England. The Liberty of Prophesying.

1909–10 Charles E. Jefferson, New York City. The Building of the Church.

1910–11 Frank W. Gunsaulus, Chicago, Illinois. The Minister and the Spiritual Life.

1911–12 J. H. Jowett, New York City. The Preacher; His Life and Work.

1912–13 Charles H. Parkhurst, New York City. The Pulpit and the Pew.

1913–14 Charles Sylvester Horne, London, England. The Romance of Preaching.

1914–15 George Wharton Pepper, Philadelphia, Pennsylvania. A Voice from the Crowd.

1915–16 William DeWitt Hyde, Brunswick, Maine. The Gospel of Good Will.

1916–17 William Fraser McDowell, Washington, D.C. Good Ministers of Jesus Christ.

1917–18 Henry Sloane Coffin, New York City. Preaching in a Day of Social Rebuilding.

1918–19 John Kelman, Edinburgh, Scotland. The War and Preaching.

1919–20 Albert Parker Fitch, Amherst, Massachusetts. Preaching and Paganism.

1920–21 Charles D. Williams, Detroit, Michigan. The Prophetic Ministry for Today.

1921–22 William Pierson Merrill, New York City. The Freedom of the Preacher.

1922–23 Charles R. Brown, New Haven, Connecticut. The Art of Preaching.

1923–24 Harry Emerson Fosdick, New York City. The Modern Use of the Bible.

1924–25 W. R. Inge, London, England. The Preaching of the Kingdom of God in Church History.

1925–26   Raymond Calkins, Cambridge, Massachusetts. The Eloquence of the Christian Experience.

1926–27   J. R. P. Sclater, Toronto, Canada. The Public Worship of God.

1927–28   James Edward Freeman, Washington, D.C. The Ambassador.

1928–29   Edwin DuBose Mouzon, Charlotte, North Carolina. Preaching with Authority.

1929–30   Francis John McConnell, New York City. The Prophetic Ministry.

1930–31   George A. Buttrick, New York City. Jesus Came Preaching.

1931–32   Ernest F. Tittle, Evanston, Illinois. Jesus After Nineteen Centuries.

1932–33   Lawrence P. Jacks, Oxford, England. Elemental Religion.

1933–34   Albert E. Day, Baltimore, Maryland. Jesus Christ and Human Personality.

1934–35   Walter Russell Bowie, New York City. The Renewing Gospel.

1935–36   J. Edgar Park, Norton, Massachusetts. The Miracle of Preaching.

INDEX